T0367305

PREVIOUS BOOKS

Healing by Contacting Your Cells.
Journal Excepts from the Ring of Fire.
What Can You Do To Help Our World?
2013 And Beyond.
2013 And Beyond Part II.
2014 World Journals.
2015 World Healing.
2015 World Healing II.
2016 World Journals.
2016 World Journals II.

http://www.globalmeditations.com

Note: http://www.globalmeditations.com opens
with the book listing giving cover photos, chapter
names, etc.

MEMORIES
2017

Barbara Wolf; Margaret Anderson

authorHOUSE®

AuthorHouse™
1663 Liberty Drive
Bloomington, IN 47403
www.authorhouse.com
Phone: 1 (800) 839-8640

Published by AuthorHouse   07/07/2017

ISBN: 978-1-5246-9836-2 (sc)
ISBN: 978-1-5246-9834-8 (hc)
ISBN: 978-1-5246-9835-5 (e)

Library of Congress Control Number: 2017910126

Photo taken by Daniel Petito at Wild Wings bird sanctuary. Jennifer Schinzing is holding Gerhard, a Great Horned Owl. Barbara is wearing a rose-colored sweater and Margaret is wearing a white sweater.

Print information available on the last page.

This book is dedicated to Barbara's husband Jack
and to the rest of the world.

Acknowlegements

David J. Adams
Masami Saionji
Hideo Nakazawa
Carmen Balhestero
Chief Golden Light Eagle
Grandmother SilverStar
Patricia Cota-Robles
Ronna Herman
Shishir Srivastava
Salwa Zeidan
Paul Winter
Hiroyoshi Kawagishi
Mitsuru Ooba
Kazuyuki Namatame
Fumi Johns Stewart
Thierry Racine and Neil Labrador
Tom and Suzie Hayes
Marco and Irene Hadjidakis
Peter and Judy Dix
Kim Reid
Annelis Kessler
Marilu Montenegro
James Tyberonn
Divino Roberto Verissimo
Yogendra Munankarmy
Stella Edmundson
Daniel Petito
Robert Ziefel
Emma Kunz
Judy Moss

FOREWORD

We firmly believe in what we believe, and we realize you may not agree with everything we believe. Probably we would not agree with everything you agree with. But let us put aside our differences and let us be friends.

It's the world that matters. Mother Earth needs help and we are trying to give it to her. That is all that is expected.

CONTENTS

Contents

INTRODUCTION

Chapter 1. We will take you to Tucson, Arizona where we will tell you about attending what is considered the greatest convention of gemstones and crystals in the world.

Chapter 2. We give you an explanation of the Unicorn, a mystical horned horse type that holds powerful healing energies. We are told to use this energy to help smooth negative energies flooding in just now. Today we have horses (without horns) that help children with special needs. We visit these horses and see them helping the special needs children.

Chapter 3. The March 20 Equinox, which many call Earth Day, is on our minds, and we want to tell you about energies coming in from outer space to help Mother Earth.

Chapter 4. We take a quick trip to Washington, D.C. to see Arlington Cemetery with its graves of over 400,000 military personnel. We ask ourselves what is the feeling here? We also go to the Basilica of Mother Mary to witness powerful positive energies.

Chapter 5. Holy Days is divided into three aspects, and we tell you about these three. Easter is the time of the Christ. Wesak is when the Christ and Buddha join forces to bring in powerful energies. The Day of Unification is June 9, Full Moon, when all are asked to unite to bring peace on Earth.

Chapter 6. We give you more discussion about Earth Day because so many are worrying about the dilemma of climate change. At the end of the chapter, Barbara briefly discuses her childhood at May Day. We also write about May Day practices in different parts of the world.

Chapter 7. We are traveling to the powerful Herkimer Sun Disc area and then to the powerful Howe Caverns. From there we travel to Concord, Massachusetts, to honor the passing of distinguished Bill Andrews.

Chapter 8. We have our minds on Alaska and the North Pole. Climate change is making the icebergs disappear. These are the homes of polar bears.

Chapter 9. We also need to tell you about Antarctica which is also experiencing climate change. A huge crack in the ice has expanded eleven miles in six days. What can we do to help Antarctica?

Chapter 10. In New York City, The Cathedral of Saint John the Divine is visited to celebrate the Summer Solstice, and also the Brooklyn Tabernacle to join with the hearts of many who are singing with Love.

CHAPTER 1

Tucson, Arizona

From Barbara:

It is February and I have just returned home from what is considered to be the greatest convention of gemstones and crystals in the world. This is at Tucson, Arizona, in the southwest part of the United States.

Since I live in the northern part of the United States, at this time of year there is snow on the ground and cold weather.

Well, Tucson is exactly opposite. There is no snow and instead of clouds, there is mostly sunshine. During the winter, the temperature can become hot during the day.

And so I have begun my travel to Tucson wearing five layers of clothes. By the time I reach Tucson, I am only wearing one layer.

For a moment, I have thoughts of staying in this paradise forever. After all, an annual big gem show begins in January and it continues until mid February. At least that is my understanding.

In any case, I am with Margaret and we arrive in February and remain in this wonderful atmosphere for five days.

Tucson is a big city. When you look at it from the sky as you fly to it, it is spread out for miles and miles and miles. On arrival, we rent a car and we first drive to the home of Tom and Suzie Hayes who have invited us to stay with them while we are in Tucson. Our friend SilverStar is staying with them and so now they have three visitors.

It isn't long before we and SilverStar are in our rental car driving to the Convention Center which we understand is the main exhibit area for the gem show. We pass a motel called Days Inn noted for its crystal displays for sale, and we are tempted to stop. But, we continue, and then we pass Howard Johnson with its big tents of gems for sale, and we do not stop. We also pass the Ramada Inn noted for having minerals and gems.

When we do reach the Convention Center, we are told that it is not opened. It will be closed for a couple days. This is a disappointment.

We decide to put our attention on nearby white-peaked tents reminding us of Native American teepees. We know these tents hold gems for sale.

One cluster has a sign saying Brazil, and this interests us. Long ago, the Atlanteans had two major crystal-growing locations, Minas Gerais in Brazil and Arkansas in USA. We have visited both places and the gems there are amazing.

Now we stop at the Brazilian white tents, and we speak with dealers from Brazil. We have a bit of difficulty understanding each other, but it is fun being with them. They show us amethyst and citrine and clear quartz and geodes of all sizes.

We are fascinated by a geode statue of huge stones holding onto each other. We ask how much this blue, aqua, and white statue costs, and the answer is $5,000. Nearby are little stones costing less than $1. Well, that difference in price means that anyone rich or poor can come here to buy.

After the gem show, when we are returning home, we change planes in Chicago. Here we meet a jewelry artist from Toronto, Canada, returning home from Tucson. She tells us she makes jewelry with gems and crystals, and she points to big bags with her. These have gems she had bought in Tucson.

We realize that the gems and crystals in Tucson that have come from all over the world are being spread throughout the world! These precious gems and crystals may not return to their homelands, but they will reside somewhere in the world!

It was wonderful seeing them in Tucson, and now, when I see exceptional artwork made from gems and crystals, I know this will remind me of my glorious visit to Tucson.

Now I want you to turn your thoughts to Margaret's trip to Tucson.

———————

From Margaret:

I am packing for Tucson, our next trip, where we will be staying with Tom and Suzie Hayes in the Oro Valley outside of Tucson during our visit to the big Tucson Gem and Mineral Show.* We will be connecting to the crystals of the world. We want to unite this powerful crystal force field to help ascend Mother Earth and all on her to higher energies.

*See Glossary: Gem and Mineral Show.

Our flight to Tucson arrives early enough for me to watch the setting sun over the desert mountains. Their power is great, and they are so approachable. They seem very loving and open to guests arriving from all over the world.

I am here in this beautiful place and I am barely grounded. The owls call. I say to the desert stones and crystals, please give me a word or two for clarity. I cannot find a grounding point. My excitement is whirling.

Margaret Channeling:

The Desert Stones and Crystals speak: Come in. Welcome. Slow down. Breathe. The air is clear here. Let your thoughts be clear. You are meeting the record keepers of the world -- the product of great changes and histories of Mother Earth -- volcanoes, Ice Ages, seas rising, sinking land rising. Fire and Ice. Can you comprehend?

Approach us with that concept. Humans are only a few decades old, but we are millions of years old. The planet is very precious. We belong to the planet. Not to the Oro Desert region, Tucson region, Arizona state, United States, North American Continent, Northern Hemisphere. We belong to Mother Earth planet without borders, without people branding us with names and values. We exist to tell the story of the planet traveling through space for millions and millions of years. And we are with her millions and millions of years. And so your petty details of life are but a flash of light and then you are gone into the whole again to return in another form and we stay constant. That is our secret. That is why we are so bright. We carry millions and millions of years of Light.

You wonder how can we carry Light when we were buried before we were found and our answer is the Light is Love expressed over time and we send our Love constantly and we send our Light constantly. So come to the Gem and Mineral Show and receive our Love and our Light and you reflect yours back to us.

With Love from Your Brothers and Sisters of the Crystalline World.

There are no differences in our world except the structure of Love -- that is what holds the particles together -- formed in space, traveling today in space, meeting one moment on a dear beloved Planet Star in space. We are but a dot of reality and in that dot is the world.

I speak, dear Brothers and Sisters of the Crystalline World, thank you for the beautiful link and understanding.

With love, Margaret

––––––––––

The next morning we drive to the crystal show with our Native American friend SilverStar. We visit the white tents of crystals. I am immediately drawn to one tent displaying a magnificent three-foot high geode with layers of blue and aqua framing a burst of clear white crystals in the center. Here I speak with Buck, a manager, and he says the crystals are from Brazil. Soon, a young man, Seth, joins us. Then a man from India joins us. I notice they are highly spiritual men who are drawn to be with us to share our Love for Mother Earth and her stones and crystals.

SilverStar tells us that Native Americans call today the Stone Nation and Crystal People Day.* How auspicious.

* See Glossary: SilverStar, The EarthStar Way Calendar.

———————

The next morning we drive to Sabino Canyon Recreation Area to ride a tram up the Sabino Canyon. This takes us along a narrow, winding road with spectacular views of high cliffs and rushing water bridges. Melting snow has filled the creeks with water and the tram has to forge on flat stone bridges that are under water. I see the water flow is very intense with strong currents and falling water. I hold tightly onto to the seat guardrails, glad for the competence of our driver-guide who navigates the rushing passageways. I see he loves the beauty and history of the canyon.

During the ascent and descent of the canyon ride, I focus on the geology of the area which is breath-taking. There are volcanic and metamorphic rock cliffs and boulders that have broken off and now lay in the streambed. Every view is different. Every view is dramatic. It is a trip one wishes to enjoy again and again.

When the ride is over, we thank the driver and go into the exhibition area to study the rock displays. Also, to see exhibits about the bird and animal wildlife and history of the early people of this area. What a delightful way to enjoy the mountains here!

Our next outing is to drive to Saguaro National Park, home of the Saguaro Cacti. These are only grown in the Sonoran Desert which is in the southern part of Arizona and California, and it extends into Mexico. The cacti here are tall, powerful, living 150 to 175 years. Their growth is slow, one inch plus the first eight years of life, and they have to be thirty-five years old to produce flowers and seventy-five years old to produce an arm.

Here in the park, the cacti cover the entire landscape unhindered by modern buildings or roads. They are in their own environment and they stately stand tall, either singly or in clusters, over vast reaches of mountainsides and valleys. Their presence is awe-inspiring. Like grand old wisdom keepers standing tall, they give a loving presence for Mother Earth.

I really want to sit and chat with them but Barbara has a mission to deliver here a sacred crystal.

———————————

From Barbara:

The cacti know what is happening. The energy is electric with anticipation. When I place a sacred crystal at the base of a tall one, all rejoice. All are happy.

———————————

From Margaret:

The next day, February 10, is when the moon crosses the shadow of Mother Earth. It is an Eclipse, a Sweet Eclipse. Father Sun tells us in Chief Golden Light Eagle's book, THE SYMBOLS, at the blinking of an eye, all things change.*

*See Glossary: Chief Golden Light Eagle, THE SYMBOLS.

The Crystals give me a message that I think I should give to you: *Rest with us in the understanding that the crystals have experienced this for millions, billions of years.*

———————————

In the early evening, we are ready to begin a Sacred Fire Ceremony to

acknowledge the Eclipse of the Full Moon. A fire is built and then SilverStar begins leading us with sacred songs and prayers.

The night is bright -- Venus is overhead and the Full Moon comes up majestically. The fire is powerful.

At the end of the ceremony, I ring the Blessings Chimes for the moon to honor it for its relationship to all the water and the flowing liquid on Mother Earth. Under the guidance of Saint Germain, David J. Adams* created these Chimes that are dedicated to healing the world's waters. David J. Adams gifted them to me.

*See Glossary: David J. Adams.

_____

Also from Margaret:

February 11, early in the morning, the owls sound and I know all is well with their world. A few hours later, we return to the crystal and gem displays to visit a tent with Pakistani pink salt blocks that will probably be made into lamps. Then we look at a three-foot pillar of amethyst crystals. I have never seen such an amazing display!

_____

Later at night, I hear an owl call close to the house. I step outside and the owl is hooting just at the side of the house. It is magical to be so close. What a blessing to have owls near by, the full moon, the mountains, the cacti, the power of this area.

A final comment: I feel it is hard to hold onto all the memories and frequencies of Tucson. Barbara says Tucson exists in higher dimensions and this is why one can feel disconnected with time and space.

I feel like an astronaut floating in a space capsule with memories whirling around me of meetings with people, happenings, and visions of beautiful sights of cacti, mountains, and crystals.

Thank you, Tucson, for showing me how it feels to live in a higher dimension and beyond. What a blessed trip!

CHAPTER 2

Animal Peace Energies

From Barbara:

As I am writing you, we are coming close to the Earth Equinox, March 20. Equal. Equal. Half of her begins Spring and the other half begins Fall. It is a moment when Mother Earth's energies are high. We learn that Arcturian Peace energies from outer space are coming in to help Mother Earth.

We are worried. There is much negative energy flooding the U.S.A. For example, our newly elected President wants to cancel a program that helps millions who cannot afford expensive health care. The conflict between the President and ordinary people becomes so great, the health care change is canceled.

We are sad this intense anger from the people comes at the same time as we are expecting great energies to come to Earth at the time of the Equinox. We want the people to have smooth tempers, and yet, we understand why they are angry. We also understand that incoming positive energies cannot function in a negative atmosphere.

We search for a solution and we remember that Saint Germain has recently told the world that the high energy of the Unicorn has begun to enter Mother Earth. This positive energy may calm matters.

In ancient times, the Unicorn was considered to be a symbol for purity of grace with the power to take poison from water and to heal sickness. My thought is that we should put the Unicorn into our minds to add it to the strongest energy of all -- LOVE.

Saint Germain also has told us that we can use our minds to create dreams and visions to help Mother Earth and humanity.

We speak with artist Michael Green who knows about the Unicorn. He says that in the Middle Ages people knew about the Unicorn, and then this knowledge grew dim. Maybe it is time for the knowledge of the Unicorn to return.

_____

From Margaret:

I ask Emma Kunz, former artist, healer from Switzerland, to channel about the Unicorn.*

*See Glossary: Emma Kunz.

Emma says: Margaret, the Unicorn is like a sunbeam, a light shaft, a rainbow of the spray of a waterfall -- fleeting, caught in the shimmering of Light. The Unicorn is opaque -- a feeling tone of companionship, an accompanier, guardian, protector, changer, charger through different dimensions.

The Unicorn reflects the finest Love frequency -- like the chalice, the sacred vessel. The Unicorn can take you to the sacred spaces -- in the deep wooded area of peace and of love.

I ask, can you find the Unicorn by the ocean?

Yes. It is found in all aspects of life.

If Barbara and I go to South America, can we take the energies of the Unicorn with us?

Yes. They are there in the ancient memories of the people in a time when people could see and be with Unicorns. Today, you cannot see them when looking for them. They appear and disappear and it is love and trust that bring them forward.

They exist more in the silence, not in music, but high flute and delicate recorder music can call them forth. Heart calling. There are other ways to call the Unicorn -- by Fragrance, Flowers, Water, Light, Crystals. The reflection of Light outward, upward, inward, all about.

Now the Unicorn comes in and speaks: *We are here. In the moment -- a view -- a sighting -- a shimmer of Light. We are answering a love call. A visit without expectations.*

More from Margaret:

I have a friend whose family background is German. For centuries, this family has had a Unicorn on its coat of arms. Emma, can you explain the meaning?

She responds: The Unicorn is very sacred -- the highest energy. The Point of Light!! The Unicorn comes to those of high frequency -- purity -- truth -- kindness and compassion. The Unicorn is of the Rainbow -- the Seal of Peace.

I realize that everyone can connect to and use the energy of the Unicorn to help the world become peaceful. Good! Just now we need this path of Purity, Truth, Kindness and Compassion.

From Barbara:

Perhaps I should add here that a physical feature of a unicorn is unique. It has a long horn that comes out of its head. In ancient times, this horn was considered so sacred, it had magical and medicinal features. If you look on the Internet you will probably find a drawing of the unicorn.

Human thought, which is energy, can merge with concepts of unicorns that have come down through the ages. A thought is creation and yet real. Some humans can actually see unicorns.

If you could conceive of a unicorn walking beside you even though it is not visible, you can conceive of Joy and Peace walking beside you. Since everything has a consciousness, including the cells of your body, wouldn't they be joyful?

———————

From Margaret:

More channeling from Emma:

Now for you, Margaret. The message is to place the Golden energy of Love around discordant energies so that they will fall away and you will hold to the Golden connections of Peace, Love and Light.

Let the storm clouds pass. Let the barriers dissolve. The greatest connection is Love -- unconditional -- given freely -- with a smile of appreciation and wonder and joy.

Let the heart live in the Garden of Love where the Unicorn lives. There, in the Garden of Love, crystals hold the essence of perfection. They hold the truth and light and love of the universes and operate on this level. We are all finally one to this understanding.

———————

From Barbara:

Although I have not yet seen a unicorn, I would be delighted to open my door and see one resting on my lawn. But, I do see today's horses, which I feel are unicorns minus their powerful front horn.

We visit from time to time a place called the EquiCenter* which brings horses together with young people with special needs. These horses are telepathic and they patiently understand the children with special needs. I call this our 'unicorn' of today. We will visit EquiCenter again.

*See Glossary: EquiCenter.

———————————

From Margaret:

When we do visit again the EquiCenter, we know we will be excited watching again therapy riding for young people with special needs.

Soon we have arranged another visit. When we leave, it is raining. But fortunately, traffic is light and we are quickly at the Volunteers Office at the EquiCenter. We wait for Karen Werth, Director of Operations, who has not yet arrived, and who will be guiding us through the therapy sessions.

While we wait, we see name badges of volunteers hanging alphabetically on the wall. We know the volunteers work with grooming and caring for horses while others assist with therapy riding sessions. All are highly trained.

The energies at the EquiCenter are strong. We like the feeling. As we wait for Karen, we pet two male cats happily curled up on tall easy chairs taking a nap.

The last time we were here, we were with Lindsay Alberts, Program Manager. Today, when she and Karen arrive, it is wonderful to be with them. Lindsay says she will be working this afternoon with a thoroughbred seven-year-old horse who was once a racehorse. She is changing him from a racehorse to a show horse.

Now we meet Smokey, a tall white horse who is with a massage therapist taking the kinks out of this horse. She says the rain has not helped Smokey's pain.

We meet a large draft horse called The Duchess, and Karen tells us this horse will work during a therapy riding session that we will watch. This very large horse has gentle eyes and an alert and inviting presence. Her color is chestnut with a black mane and tail. A volunteer is bridling her as another volunteer is placing on her back blankets held in place by a wide, strong leather strap.

When we are ready to watch the therapy session, a young man, a teenager, arrives to ride The Duchess bareback. Karen tells us that riding bareback will help develop his core muscles and strengthen his coordination. Three volunteers will be with him -- two side walkers and a horse leader.

Karen also tells us the rider needs to be alert to instructions, including the horse's gate. And, he must be aware of markers, hanging Frisbees, posted letters, etc.

We notice that when the young man has first arrived, his face is without expression, as if he is unaware of where he is.

The volunteers begin to ground him by walking him beside the horse and a volunteer walks beside him, both holding a rope to the horse. When the young man is considered grounded, he is told to mount the horse bareback.

He mounts, and the horse begins walking. Now the young man is told to lift his arms up, then out to his sides, and then over his head. We know this will help develop his muscles and strengthen his coordination.

We know we are both watching the horse bring peace and stability to the young man. Here is an animal, a horse, who graciously gives itself to helping humanity.

When the horse approaches a Frisbee hanging on a rope attached to the ceiling, the young man is told to lift up his arm and catch the Frisbee and throw it into a bucket. At first he misses the bucket, but when he is told to reach for another Frisbee and throw it into a bucket, he succeeds. The volunteers cheer his success! Karen, who is with us, notes these exercises will also sharpen his eye-hand coordination.

As we watch, we feel the young man is responding more and more to the trainers. When he and the horse are close to us, we smile at him to show him our joy at his accomplishment. He smiles back.

We note that the three enthusiastic volunteers are smiling at him as they cheer him on, and we know the smiling and cheering is part of the lesson. It will take time for this young man to change, but we know the horses and volunteers will change him.

Karen explains to us that the gait of a horse is the same as that of a human. Therefore, humans having difficulty walking or having poor coordination will settle into the walking gait of the horse. After riding, this facilitates walking by themselves.

Riding also stimulates vocal capacities. When young people have difficulty speaking, they will, after riding, begin talking first to the horse and then to people.

What a gift horses give!

Karen tells us a deep bond of friendship and love forms between the rider and the horse.

_____

From Barbara:

Margaret has told you about our fantastic journey to EquiCenter where horses give to children with special needs.

Here is a project involving EquiCenter that does not include horses. It involves people selflessly giving military veterans confidence to live normal lives. Today we are told there is a silent epidemic of suicides among U.S. Veterans unable to normally re-enter civilian society.

EquiCenter has hired veteran Tim Braley to work at the Center but horses will not be his main focus here. He is in charge of teaching veterans how to plant crops, grow them, harvest them and how to cook them for food.

I know these veterans will never hear a sour word. They will work in a kitchen called "Dream Kitchen" where there is always laughter and joy. This warm and friendly atmosphere would be good for the nation's heroes to put aside the depression and horror of war.

Within a few miles of EquiCenter is a very large Canandaigua Veterans Medical Center housing military veterans. Some living there have been connected to EquiCenter to participate in the food program.

Margaret and I have had personal volunteer experiences at the hospital. Yearly, just before Christmas, volunteers are invited to come to the hospital, wear Christmas hats and join groups of veterans living at the hospital.

One time I was with veterans who, as expected, were talking about war experiences. One man told us about flying his helicopter over Viet Nam. He did not speak about personal violence, but when he spoke, I felt he was with his buddies at war.

One expressionless man sat by himself without speaking. I stood beside him stroking his hair and giving his forehead little kisses. He showed no emotion, and I continued doing this until it was time to leave. Then he looked at me and I could see his eyes wanted me to stay. His mouth could not speak, but his eyes spoke.

I am happy that EquiCenter is addressing the veterans' epidemic of silence. I hope there are many, many organizations across the world helping to stop this epidemic.

_____

More from Barbara:

I want to end this chapter by continuing a bit longer about animals. Margaret and I decide to visit the Seneca Park Zoo to see animals of the world, especially those coming from Africa. I know the zoo has two elephants from Africa, and the zoo's lions and tigers may be from Africa.

My thought is that just now Africa is experiencing a big drought. Millions of people living there are contending with not enough food to eat because of the drought. If African humans have a problem with the drought, then animals living there are also having a problem. Their food supply is also reduced.

What can be done to help the animals?

When we visit the zoo today, I know the animals here are well fed. There is no drought to shorten the food supply. I cannot help thinking about their brothers and sisters facing drought in Africa.

When I was a child, I remember traveling with my family to visit relatives living fourteen and more hour's drive from our home. To break the boredom of such a long journey, we would play a game of counting horses and cows in the fields along the way. Each cow and horse was a certain count. Whoever in the car had the largest count won the game. When one game was over, we would start again.

Well, today, horses and cows do not populate the fields in such large numbers as before. As for the zoo Margaret and I visit, we see no cows and horses. However, we do see two elephants, and their enclosure is so close to our walkway, we are able to come very close to them. We are certain they are well fed.

As a last remark, we feel the animals are happy here at the zoo. I would be happy if this happiness extended throughout the world. We would have peace, and maybe the unicorns would like to openly visit again.

Chapter 3

March Equinox

From Barbara:

We need to prepare for March 20, a date many call Earth Day. It is a moment when Mother Earth is balanced. Half of her begins Spring and the other half begins Fall. It is the Equinox!

Happy Birthday, Mother Earth!

In celebration, peace bells are rung throughout the world. The United Nations in New York City is one peace bell ringing location. That is where we expect to be at the Equinox, but a last-minute development changes our plans. Heavy snow and ice in New York City. We cancel.

We know that at the moment of the Equinox, equal, equal, Mother Earth energies will be very high.

We are told that energies are already coming in from Outer Space. In particular, we are told special energies called Arcturian Peace Energies are coming in. Arcturus is Mother's Earth brother in the sky joining with other energies to help her during this rugged time.

Just before March 20, I am staggered, unbalanced by enormous power! Every moment, I need to watch my step.

I am not tired. I have plenty of energy to work continually throughout the day to prepare for the Equinox, but I am staggered.

Margaret and I review the meaning of the energies coming from Arcturus. These are collections of energies from different parts of the Universe. How wonderful that so many of Mother Earth's brothers and sisters are trying to help her!

From Australia we learn that energy lines called Songlines* will be heavily involved with the March Equinox. These Songlines circle the Earth and one penetrates Serpent Mound, which is important at the time of the Equinox. The energy there will be particularly enhanced.

*See Glossary: Songlines.

————————

From Margaret, channeling excepts about the Equinox:

The Equinox brings all life into balance. The planet is straight up with equal day and equal night. The moment of perfection.

Balance, balance, balance for Mother Earth and all systems.

Love can move mountains. It cannot be taken away. It is always there, the eternal spring well within the heart.

————————

Still from Margaret:

To know more, I need to connect with the serpent of Serpent Mound, so important at the Spring Equinox. *

*See Glossary: Serpent Mound.

I say, dear serpent of Serpent Mound, what is the meaning of the great moment of the Equinox when the Earth planet is in perfect balance?

What is your role in all of this?

Serpent responds: I come from the past to greet the future. You stand in the now and ask the question. My power is ancient. My energy flows through the dimensions. You can open every door and I am there in creativity, in creation. That is why I am such a holy place for the opening of the door to Spring where Mother Earth is in perfect balance and my contour delineates each sacred moment of her travels, her position in space, the tilt of the axis, the relationship / view of the sun at sunrise.

All is energy. I am beneath and on top of the energy. My concept projects the energy of life's power. I am a self-contained unit and I connect with all. So you see there is no separation between me and Songlines continents away. We are all connected by the current lines of the planet.

The human noise/thought level, mechanical thinking approach to life needs to be softened, dampened down. Can you hear the leaf fall from a tree?

Can you hear the tulip grow? Can you hear the rustle of the baby bird in its nest?

There are so many melodies, sounds of Nature. The snake moves easily over Mother Earth's surface. The snake is at one with Mother Earth and so there is no friction. The snake is the guardian of energy lines -- the Songlines. Each part of the snake picks up the deep, powerful energies of Mother Earth, and with Mother Earth, gathers and sends out the power.

I see, Margaret, you are fascinated by the coil of my tail -- the power base that springs forward -- the coil that can project energy through space.

Take on the awareness of the Serpent that reflects the elements of land, air, water, fire. Here is where we merge into a vaster concept of the Dragon Lines, the Water Veins. We are guardians of the elements. Humans too should be guardians. They are too busy slicing and dicing the earth's surface. Let each action begin with an in-breath of gratitude and an out-breath of prayer and gratitude.

Sit in your travels going here, going there, and acknowledge the presence, the dignity, the wonder of this amazing planet full of beauty and wonder.

If only the people's heads were on the ground as ours are, then they can move across the surface and be aware of the planet -- the internal condition, the psyche, the heart, the soul of the great Planet Earth. We move and every rib touches Mother Earth and registers her frequency.

From Barbara:

In the sky high above us is a star cluster called Draco, known as the Great Dragon. It is my understanding that under the influence of the great dragon Draco, a meteor fell from the sky and landed on Mother Earth to form Serpent Mound. This influence of Draco remains forever.

Therefore, when there is an important happening concerning Mother Earth, such as the March 20, 2017 Equinox event bringing in Arcturian Peace Energy, this is recorded in the history books of Draco, the dragon.

From Margaret:

I channel to Draco:

We are approaching the sacred moment of the Equinox and we know the serpent of Serpent Mound is important. Are you the overseer? Can you comment?

Draco responds: I am the hidden power behind the Serpent Mound, the energy beneath and above. I am visible and invisible. My power, visible and invisible. One should present a frequency of reverence approaching my domain.

I am robust, fiery, electrical -- all the attributes to start and enhance life, especially in reference to the seeds and water.

Draco energy is expressed through the dragon as the guardian of the sacred water fountains in Japan that are guarded by fierce dragon energies presented as dragon spouts. The power is not diminished when transferred over distance. It is planted and contained in the sacred wells, springs, mounds, waterways.

Meteors can bring my power to Earth which is registered by the hearts of those who think on me.

So many lines of thought are coming together at Serpent Mound echoing those who support Mother Earth at this amazing, powerful Equinox, March 20, 6:29 a.m. All hearts are joined and linked together across the world as I, Draco, view from above.

Draco.

From Barbara:

There are twelve major energy lines called Songlines on this planet and all will receive the Arcturian Peace Energy gifted to Mother Earth. At the moment though, we are considering the Songline energy going to Mount Kailash, located in Tibet.

What is the importance of Mount Kailash?

It is the gateway for penetrating consciousness. Without consciousness, the Divine Purpose just now would be meaningless.

We know that consciousness leads to awareness. This will lead to enlightenment. Enlightenment leads to Peace.

Mount Kailash, when it is stimulated by the energy of Peace, will allow the new energy of peace to come in with a consciousness for Mother Earth. That is of prime importance. The consciousness of peace energy will allow the peace energy to become a reality. Without consciousness, it goes nowhere.

And so, at the Equinox there is a need for a consciousness to stimulate the awareness of the peace energies flowing.

While this is being done at the Equinox, the Higher Worlds will help.

––––––––––

From Margaret:

I channel asking for more understanding of the Universal Law of Consciousness, and I receive:

The Universal Law of Consciousness is the opening of the reception of information on all levels (mental, physical, spiritual, emotional) and in all dimensions and realities.

This opening of Consciousness is to be aware of the feelings, thoughts, emotions, physical being of others -- humans, plants, trees, water, rock, fire, air. To have a clear ability to understand someone's situation, which means to have the ability to walk in someone else's shoes.

You would be compassionate singularly and universally.

You would expand your geographic thinking of your neighborhood to include the hemisphere, planet, solar system, universe, universes.

You would have all families be your family.

You would avoid separation and barriers. All are one. How can you divide the air space, the flow of the water, the strength of the land? The environment belongs to everyone and needs to be cherished and maintained in its original state of perfection.

Consciousness needs to be expanded to comprehend the vast complexities of all life systems -- how they are interconnected and vibrant. The love of this understanding enhances all life forms and encourages generosity of the Spirit.

―――――――

From Barbara:

For the Equinox, we still need to prepare more. We print out a photograph of the world from space. And then, a powerful photograph of Serpent Mound, plus a photograph of Mount Kailash.

We locate on the computer a chorus of 10,000 in Japan joyously singing Ode to Joy.* We listen, and yes, this singing is compatible with peace energies sent to Mother Earth by the Arcturians.

*See Glossary: Ode to Joy.

WE ARE READY for the Equinox. And, I need to add here that we will not be at Serpent Mound. We will at home base.

―――――――

Now comes a surprise:

We have just learned that the Maoris of New Zealand have arrived at Serpent Mound. They are representatives of ancient times of Mother Earth. Our opinion is that these ancient people are ready to lose their homeland. Changes have brought continuous earthquakes to New Zealand. A new continent has been discovered under the surface. There is much we do not know about what is happening in New Zealand.

―――――――

March 20, 6:29 a.m., moment of the Equinox, we are playing Musical Rapture* and the volume is very soft. There is a reason for selecting this music. At one point, the Angels begin singing. Their energy is coming from dimensions higher than our third dimension. With our minds, we connect the higher Angelic dimensions to the energy coming to Mother Earth from the Arcturians. We are stimulating this peace energy.

AUM.

*See Glossary: Musical Rapture.

From Margaret:

We light incense and the incense floats sweetly in the room as we begin playing Musical Rapture, the divine love music. I hold my quartz crystal from southern France as I begin my meditation. In my mind, I connect to the Songlines and I focus on Mount Kailash as Light. I am enveloped by radiant crystalline golden white Light. In that Light, I focus on receiving the peace frequencies of the Arcturians.

Now I move to Japan and I breathe in the bliss of JOY of the Japanese 10,000 singers singing Ode to Joy. I realize that JOY IS LOVE IN ACTION.

I move across the world to The Brooklyn Tabernacle singers expressing Joy of Faith and Universal LOVE -- a fountain that embraces the world. Then I follow the Love Frequencies to Christ and to Mary. My meditation is all about Consciousness -- Light Expansion. The Perfection of Mother Earth. Peace on Earth.

AUM.

From Barbara, one day later:

We need to thank the 10,000 Japanese who have sung Ode to Joy. The energy field of singing was ENORMOUS yesterday.

We know it doesn't matter whether the singing was five years ago, last year, or whenever. We have entered the energy field and it is as powerful as the day the 10,000 sang Ode to Joy.

To thank them, we decide to go to The Plum Garden, a Japanese restaurant that is so energized with Japanese energy, one feels as if one is eating in Japan. We select Japanese food and we watch Japanese cooks preparing the food within fifty feet of us.

Again, thank you 10,000 singers, for giving us the energy to help Mother Earth at the Equinox.

CHAPTER 4

Washington, D.C.

From Barbara:

April 7, we go to Washington D.C.

Why?

We need to visit Arlington Cemetery that has the graves of over 400,000 military personnel and their families. Throughout the year, many more are buried here, and, in addition, there are yearly over 3,000 ceremonies and memorial services.

We need to honor those buried there. Our planet is ascending from the third dimension to higher dimensions. All associated with her are ascending, including those buried here. What is the feeling of big Arlington? Are the vibrations here good or are they not good?

The second reason why we are visiting Washington, D.C. is to feel the vibrations of the capital of our country. Recently there have been disruptions and marches, etc. Is the capital tranquil or is it feeling the disruptions?

Another reason to visit Washington, D. C. just now is to go to the Mother Mary place called the Basilica of the National Shrine of the Immaculate Conception. This place has very powerful positive energies.

We quickly prepare ourselves for flying to Washington, D.C., but, to our dismay, there is snow on the ground and more coming! Also, there is heavy fog!

Will planes be flying? We will soon know. Our taxi driver is due to pick us up at 10 a.m., and usually the taxi is fifteen minutes early.

9:45 a.m. comes and goes and the driver has not arrived. We phone and we are told he will be a bit late. 10 a.m. comes and goes and the driver still has not arrived. We phone again and we are told he will be coming soon.

Yes, he comes and we pile our bags and ourselves into the taxi for the driver to promptly begin taking us to the airport. BUT,,,,,now we learn his orders are to take us to the train! Well, fortunately he drives a short way and we realize the airport has not been in his thoughts. When we tell him we are going to the airport, he quickly changes his plans. He does, however, show us his iPad that has orders for going to the train station!

This is a small hiccup at the beginning of our journey. Will we have more?

In any case, we do reach the airport, and we do go through Security with many, many others. When we reach our gate for the plane to Washington, D.C., a second hiccup is ready to happen.

The weather is so bad, and especially the fog is so heavy, incoming pilots are not landing to pick up their next passengers. An announcer is broadcasting to many potential passengers that their Chicago-bound plane is overhead but not landing. The pilot does not trust landing in the fog, and so he decides to land elsewhere. Good-bye, Chicago-bound passengers.

Will the announcer begin broadcasting anything about the plane coming in to take us to Washington D.C.? Yes! We are told that the pilot is nearly here to land, but, will he land? We sit and wait near nervous airline personnel at the departure desk.

We are all wondering if he will land.

YES!

The nervous airline personnel clap!

And so, yes, the pilot lands and we quickly are told to begin boarding. Within minutes, the plane, a small one, takes off with a mighty roar. My thought is that the pilot is an ex-military pilot used to landing in unfavorable weather.

Our flight is quick, a little over an hour from start to finish, and at Ronald Reagan Washington National Airport we are taken by bus to the American Airlines terminal where we hire a taxi to the Capitol Skyline Hotel which will be our weekend home.

At the hotel's front desk, we are greeted by personnel who, after we request a room with a direct view of the nation's capitol building, phone the hotel cleaning staff to ask if there are any room vacancies with the view. Yes, if we wait about fifteen minutes for a room being cleaned.

And so we wait patiently with hope in our hearts and yes, we are given room 414 which directly faces the capitol building.

I find it interesting that our hotel's name, the Capitol Skyline Hotel, reflects this famous building.

And I want to mention here that my first impression of Washington today is that the energy feels jagged, not smooth. I think too many recent unexpected happenings have affected the energy.

April 8, Saturday:

Still from Barbara:

Early morning, I am standing at the hotel window watching sunlight bringing a bright glow to the capitol building. I am noting that we will have good weather today!

We eat breakfast in the dining room, and this breakfast is free! Jesse, a hotel manager, has given us free tickets! He is a gracious man with a big smile who reflects the warm smiles coming from all the hotel personnel.

Jesse tells us that a shuttle bus is outside the hotel door and this bus will take us free to wherever we want to go more or less within the hotel area. A metro map is in our hands, and we tell the driver we want to go to a metro line that will connect us with a metro line going to the Arlington stop.

Yes, yes, of course, the driver says, and we are soon on our way as he is telling us that many streets are closed because a big cherry blossom parade will soon begin this morning. He knows how to avoid the closed streets, and just as we are approaching our metro, we cross a big boulevard closed to traffic. We look down this closed street and we see big, bright, colorful balloons ready to be paraded down the boulevard. Hundreds are already assembling to watch the parade.

At the metro stop, we use an escalator to go downstairs to reach a uniformed man standing next to a machine for buying tickets. We want to buy one ticket that can handle all metro rides for today and tomorrow, and this man patiently explains the approximate cost. Then he takes my money and inserts it into the machine and out comes a stiff card called M Smartrip enclosed in a sleeve advertising the National Cherry Blossom Festival, March 20-April 16, 2017.

When Margaret has her ticket, we walk a few feet to the turnstiles, but, where do we insert the ticket? Fortunately, the uniformed man has remained with us because he realizes we are unfamiliar with the metro. He shows us where to put our yellow cards, and he helps us place our new cards on a bright-colored symbol at the turnstile. This opens for us to enter and go to the metro train. How amazing this new system is!

Now we reach the metro tracks and we read signs telling us which metro to take. Within a few minutes, our metro arrives and stops for us. We enter and we are soon moving slowly along.

When we reach the Arlington Cemetery stop, we hail a taxi to take us around the cemetery. But, this changes to only a couple minutes with him because he takes us to building where we can become part of a shuttle adventure of going 60 minutes around the cemetery.

We climb aboard and we quickly learn that the shuttles today are loaded with chaperoned groups of students who have come to Arlington for the weekend of the Cherry Blossom Festival. They are all having a wonderful time.

The shuttle driver drives us slowly along as he speaks via a microphone to tell us what and where to look. Occasionally he stops for riders to get off and they will get on another shuttle later.

What is my opinion of Arlington Cemetery? IT IS HUGE. I have seen photographs of the cemetery but it is MUCH MUCH MUCH LARGER than the photographs show. We travel slowly along by shuttle for an hour and we have hardly 'touched' what is here.

The place is clean. One does not see any trash or any discarded paper.

The MANY MANY tombstones are clean, as if they have been washed today.

The vibrations are calm as if the soldiers beneath the tombs are resting in peace. This is certainly unlike a Japanese cemetery I visited several years ago where warriors under the ground were continuing with military practices.

Yes, the vibrations at Arlington Cemetery are good. Calm and peaceful.

After the shuttle ride, Margaret and I leave Arlington Cemetery to take a metro to the Mother Mary place called the Basilica of the National Shrine of the Immaculate Conception. We arrive at noon with lunch on our minds, knowing that our desire for food will be fulfilled. Just inside the door is a long eating area with tables and chairs for many. And yes, many are hungry, too. We choose a table for eating, and then we join others buying food at the restaurant's food display. I buy bean soup and mix the soup with beans cooked into the form of a pastry. Delicious! This is the first time for me to mix soup with pastry.

When we finish lunch, we begin walking through the Basilica that can hold 10,000 people and has over seventy chapels honoring Mother Mary. In particular, I like the Byzantine-Ruthenian Chapel. This is a colorful chapel that commemorates Mary's intervention in 626 A.D. in a church in Constantinople where people were gathered to pray to be saved from the enemy. The belief is that Mary appeared and saved them by protecting them with her mantle.

What is so impressive about the Basilica is the absence of negativity. We realize the powerful positive energy here can be joined with today's major positive event in the nation's capital, the Cherry Blossom Festival. Yes, Washington, D.C. feels good today. The negative energy sitting here yesterday has faded.

———————————

April 9:

We have time this morning to visit the Cherry Blossom Festival before flying out of Washington, D.C. this afternoon. The best place to see cherry blossoms would be at the Tidal Basin. And, with great expectations, we take a taxi to this place. But, the Tidal Basin is a disappointment. There are no cherry blossoms. They have been torn off the trees by a tremendous windstorm. Some trees have been knocked over and their huge roots are pointing upward toward the sky. I have never seen anything like this.

Interesting, some redbud trees are here and they are in full bloom. Maybe they were not in blossom until after the storm and so the blossoms have been saved from doom.

When it is time to fly out of Washington, D.C., we take a taxi to the airport to fly home.

Good-bye, Washington D.C. We enjoyed visiting you.

_____

From Margaret:

April 7:

Barbara has already explained how our flight begins with dense fog and snow. We are happy when the sky opens above Washington, D.C. Throughout our journey, weather is no longer a problem.

We take a taxi to Capitol Skyline Hotel where we are given a perfect room with a direct view of the Capitol Building. We can see it through the large window.

To give positive energy to Washington, D.C., I place the Vortexes* at the window.

*See Glossary: Vortexes.

I ring the Blessings Chimes for Washington, D.C. and I place them on the window ledge with a picture of Christ, Mary, and Bawa Muhaiyaddean, a Sufi Mystic.*

*See Glossary: Bawa Muhaiyaddean.

I also place on the window ledge a photograph of the Statue of Freedom* that is at the top of the Capitol Building.

*See Glossary: Statue of Freedom.

My efforts are to give positive energy to the nation's capital, Washington, D.C.

In the evening when the night lights go on, we watch the Capitol Building being lighted. Our room is perfect. The building is always in our gaze.

April 8:

At sunrise, Barbara asks me which of the twenty-two Star Law Symbols would I place over Washington, D.C. right now to give positive energy to the city. I say the Symbol is the Universal Law of Love -- the greatest power of all.

We meditate and we place Love over all of Washington, D. C., and then we send out Love world wide. We want Washington to be ruled mainly by the heart, not just mainly by the head.

After meditation, I ring the Blessings Chimes for the sunrise over the Capitol Building, the city, the country and the world.

When it is time for breakfast, we go to the dining room on the first floor to enjoy a delicious meal. And then it is time to go to Arlington. A shuttle driver begins taking us to the Metro, and on the way, I see a young tree who begins to speak with me.

He says: I am a Tree of Love. Each branch grows carrying Love. Each branch grows, extends, and expands Love and gives Love again to the other branches coming. This represents Love given through all the generations. I am a Tree of Love. Consider this when viewing all trees.

We take the Metro to Arlington Cemetery and here we ride a long tram which slowly moves us up steep hills. We see trees and soft green grass filled with parallel rows of grave markers of military service people who have served in every war. It is sobering to see the vastness of the graves. This was once Robert E. Lee's house and property, and now it is the National Cemetery for those who served the country in the military.

The tram makes stops so people can get out and view different tombs -- the JFK gravesite, The Tomb of the Unknown Soldier, different monuments. What catches my eye is not actually in the cemetery. It is the United States Air Force Memorial located on the grounds of Fort Myers adjacent to Arlington. This memorial consists of three spires curving up, representing Thunderbird jets flying in formation, honoring those who have served in the Air Force.

We see the graves of Civil War soldiers from the North and from the South.

The day is cold and crisp with bright sunshine. Young and old are on the tram. Many are visiting Arlington to visit their loved ones and to bring love to those who served. Each has a life, a story, a family, a place, and all are gathered here because they served their country in the military. Love is pouring out to the many thousands buried here.

We then go to the magnificent church dedicated to Mary, the Basilica of the National Shrine of the Immaculate Conception. When we are reaching her church, we walk among beautiful flowering trees and tulips and other bright spring flowers.

Before visiting the many chapels to Mary inside the church, we have lunch sitting near the stained glass window of Christ and two disciples sitting at a table.

Afterward, we visit the Orthodox Chapel, the Byzantine Ruthenian Chapel where Mary rescued the people in a Constantinople church with her mantle.

I think we should wrap the city of Washington, D. C. with Mary's blessed scarf. Also, let us wrap her scarf around those buried in Arlington as well as around the entire world.

In the Basilica, I walk upstairs to the Virgin of Guadalupe Chapel where I pray for my family and the healing of all families. Then I go to the Blessed Sacrament Chapel on the side of the main altar. Here, I think about Christ's entry into Jerusalem, and I feel Christ's entry here, in this city, in Washington, D. C. I feel enveloped by Christ's Love and I pour this Love over Washington, D.C. and over the entire planet.

———————

It is now 8:30 p.m. and I am in our Capitol Skyline Hotel room writing up my notes. I feel the city seems smoother. It is shining. I feel the Love vibration has settled on the city's frequency.

———————

April 9:

We watch the Sunrise focusing on the Statue of Freedom on the top of the dome of the Capitol Building. The day is greeted by the Statue of Freedom wearing a Native American headdress with an eagle on top.

The morning light has changed from bright gold to silvery white Light.

———————

8:45 a.m., we take a taxi to see the cherry blossoms at the Tidal Basin which is close to the Jefferson Memorial and the Lincoln Memorial. But, as Barbara has already told you, the Tidal Basin has experienced a terrible tornado that has uprooted and damaged many trees.

When we drive around the Tidal Basin, we see the tornado damage. Few cherry trees have blossoms but most are gone.

We have passed a stone Japanese lantern honoring the gift of cherry trees from Japan to the United States in 1912. Lighting this lantern opens the Cherry Blossom Festival.

May Peace Prevail On Earth.

May the Frequency of Washington, D. C. be transformed into Peace, Love, and Light.

We have had a glorious visit to Washington, D. C.!

CHAPTER 5

Holy Days
Easter, Wesak, Unification

Easter

From Barbara:

For many, this is a holy time of the year. Hearts are sending out positive energies of love and thanksgiving. Easter is in April, the time of the Christ. Wesak is in May, the time of the Buddha and the Christ. June is the time of Unification.

To help the world, Margaret and I want to take advantage of this outpouring of positive energy.

For April, what can we do?

We put our thoughts together and we decide to send positive energies to the continent of Africa which is experiencing great drought. The land is too dry for crops to survive and the United Nations estimates that 14 million people face starvation. Food has become very expensive to buy and so many families are depending on eating only one meal a day.

Yes, we want to help ease this problem.

Big Lake Ontario is close to where we live. This is connected to five big lakes to make the biggest fresh water source in the world. We decide to go to this big fresh water source to stimulate energies to help bring water/rain to Africa.

We will have with us a map of Africa and a large photograph of water and a picture of the Christ. When we reach the lake, we will throw into the water the picture of the Christ to stimulate the thought form of water being sent to drought-stricken Africa.

When we reach Lake Ontario, we enter Durand Eastman Park and stop near a long pier that goes out to a lighthouse. We step out of the car and walk onto the pier to an area where we can look down to see ducks in the water waiting for food to be thrown to them. Well, no ducks are waiting today.

But, there is a bit of wind and I am beginning to worry about the Christ picture which is in my hand. When it hits the water, will it turn over and the Christ will be facing downward?

I do not want the Christ to face downward.

I throw in the Christ picture, and it hits the water face up. Good! Then I watch as one edge begins to curl. But, there is a pause and the curl stops. The Christ remains face up.

WONDERFUL!!!!!

We say to the Christ, who seems to be looking at us, that Africa needs water. Please help make this happen.

We stay a few moments looking down at him, waiting for him to submerge himself, but no, he remains looking up at us.

Good-bye, Christ, we say as we leave him.

———————

Now here is some stunning news.

A couple days later we receive an email from a friend living in Africa. He lives in the country of Uganda.

Our friend's email says it is raining and there is some relief! He says the drought has affected everyone, but maybe that is finished and the people can begin planting food.

———————

From Margaret:

Easter message from the Christ:

Dear Margaret, I see humanity is in a quandary, a distress over the uncertainty of the future. So many areas are under conflict -- countries are split between peoples. I feel the people call out for help. It seems everything is unresolvable.

Before beginning, place a force field over the situation and invite those opposing each other to come together in silence to pray together for peace. Lay out the reality of war -- a conflict that in the end no one wins. Only suffering and pain wins.

The key is to bring to the table those in conflict to witness the other -- to hear the suffering -- to look at those who suffer on both sides. Rushing into conflict creates chaos -- problems that need to be solved delicately in deliberation. To escalate will cause great damage and civilization is sent backwards. There is unanimity in wanting peace -- to come to a peaceful resolution before conflict begins. This is imperative.

Acts of kindness, the gift of flowers, the acknowledging of each other's work -- that changes the vibration and gives breathing room, space for peace to be accomplished.

Barbara Wolf; Margaret Anderson

It takes a short moment to explode a place and generations to heal the consequences.

————————

The gift of Easter day is that the people are in a thankful state -- seeing a different reality that life continues. It does not end. The spring flowers and the trees in spring that bloom rejoice in this message of life continuing.

Look at the long view. Spread peace in your mind as you approach the day, the week, the month. Do not get caught in a downdraft of fear. Hold your focus steady. Be loving. Be joyful. Be of good will.

At the core, people are basically good. When approaching them as good people, they will respond. Send out a positive energy field. Expand your Light. Expand your Love. Embrace the work of devoted people as you did when you embraced the work of the devoted people at the Call Center in the Veterans Hospital.

The building blocks of a vibrant society are when all are equal and share in the effort of rebuilding, creativity, affirming life, bringing people together, working together, sharing, laughing, smiling, encouraging.

When people work together, it is not so hard to build a project. Building peace. Building communities. Supporting Nature and the natural systems. All are interrelated.

————————

This is the Way of the Orchid. It is fragile and delicate and yet a powerful force field of healing and goodwill. The angels come down through the orchids. Prayers go out through the orchids. They are great healers.

Give love to everyone at Easter, and when you look at chaos, return it to calm.

May peace be with you.

The Christ.

More from Margaret:

Via email, Barbara and I send pictures of delicate lilies to our friends living in all the continents of the world -- North America, South America, Europe, Asia, Australia, India.

Today I see a Rainbow Ring around the Sun. A gift! I have only seen four in my lifetime -- in Brazil, in Japan, at the local reservoir, and now on a local road I see a Rainbow Ring around the Sun.

I am stunned! To me, this is a HOLY SIGHT. To me, it means PEACE.

There are rumblings of war and the world is on edge.

Thank you, dear Sun. Thank you, dear Mother Earth, for this Special Sign of PEACE.

Later comes another acknowledgment of Peace -- a young bald eagle flying over the car.

On Easter Day, the Higher Worlds say we are to deliver an orchid to the Call Center at the Canandaigua Veterans Hospital. We buy an orchid, but before leaving, we print out ten big pictures of lilies that we want to give out. The first one goes to the woman attendant at the Thruway tollbooth and she is delighted. Rather than a standard half-smile, which is expected when toll money is given to her, she reacts with joy when receiving the picture of the lilies.

Our hearts are full of Joy and Love as we drive along, and our minds are on countering the negativity of war rumblings and disputes. We want humanity to come together to live in Peace and Love.

At the hospital we are cheerfully greeted as we give out the orchid and the lily photographs.

When we leave the hospital, we drive a short way to the historic site of Ganondagan where a great peace tree is sending out peace energies. We stop at this tree to place our prayers for peace.

Wesak

From Barbara:

I think May 10, 2017 is the most important Buddhist celebration of the year. This celebration always happens on the full moon of Taurus. Today, the full moon of Taurus is in the month of May, and sometimes it is in the month of June. Where I live in New York State, the exact moment of the full moon is May 10, 2017, 5:42 p.m.

The Buddhist celebration today is called the Wesak Festival and it celebrates the Taurus full moon birth in the Far East of the one called Buddha. Also, it is believed that Buddha died on the full moon of Taurus at the age of 80, and today He remains in the Higher Worlds.

It is believed that every year at the exact moment of the full moon of Taurus, the energy of Buddha will return in full force.

Where?

In a remote Himalayan area, and thousands yearly go to the Himalayas to join others who have also gone there.

Buddha will not be seen, but the energy He brings to earth at this time will be ENORMOUS.

Another belief of great importance is that at the moment of the full moon today, the Christ will join His energies with Buddha's energies for the radiating of great energies throughout the world.

Again, Buddha will not be seen and the Christ will not be seen.

It should be noted that the enormous energies they will be sending down to the earth are for everyone regardless of faith.

As we all know, there is much chaos on our planet just now. We all want peace. We all want joy. On this special day, let us open our hearts to thoughts of peace and joy.

———————

I want to add here that this powerful energy combination of the Christ and Buddha is for everything in the world. For humanity, yes, but also for the animals and the birds and Nature. Everything living on this planet is given energy.

I live in an area of many, many apple trees. To grow apples, the trees need to be fertilized by bees. In recent years, less and less bees have been doing this work, and now beekeepers are bringing them in boxes to fertilize the apple orchards.

A few months ago, I learn that south of where I live millions of honeybees have been killed because of acute pesticide poisoning in South Carolina to get rid of Zika mosquitoes.

The bees cannot speak for themselves. At Wesak, when big energy is coming to our world, I concentrate the Christ/Buddha energy on Nature, and this includes the bees.

I also concentrate on the birds. Especially the Bald Eagles dying because they are poisoned by eating dead animals shot by hunters using lead bullets.

This poisoning affects the nervous systems of the eagles so they become paralyzed and cannot fly. The muscles and brain are affected and some eagles can no longer stand or hold up their heads. Some cannot open their beaks.

Yes, I concentrate on the Christ/Buddha energy coming to this world to help all living on it. I remember the plight of the eagles and all other birds affected by lead poisoning.

And I do not forget the geese. Every year flocks of them fly in the fall from their northern Canadian homes to their southern Florida homes. My joy is hearing them calling each other as they fly.

Last year, a flock of about fifty geese stopped flying south when they reached a big lake near me. When the water turned to ice, they stayed on the ice rather then on the land. My thought is that staying on the ice protects them from predators, especially in the dark of night.

Well, a year ago in the winter, we had a tremendous storm that brought heavy amounts of snow. I worried about the geese living on the ice of the frozen lake. Did they survive the storm?

I went to the lake, and YES, they were still on the frozen lake!

Just now, it is the first part of the month of May and I am writing you about Wesak, the big Christ/Buddha event. I am not hearing the calling of geese as they fly from the warm South to their homes in the North.

I am hearing nothing. Where are they?

At Wesak, I use Christ/Buddha energy as I pray that the geese are safe.

_____

PS: Kim, a friend living in Canada near the US border just north of me emails she has heard geese calling. Well, that is a joy to me. I hope many geese will begin flying from south to north.

_____

From Margaret;

I ask, what is the meaning of Wesak, and I receive channeling:

It is the time of the full moon of Taurus -- the holy time of Buddha's birth and reappearance in the high Himalayas in the sacred valley where all gather to receive His blessing.

This day, the event is a doorway in time to open the dimensions where love, compassion and fortitude can be dispersed to those gathered and those around the world gathered in thought, in spirit.

I am told:

With the mind, in meditation, travel to the high mountains of the Himalayas. Journey to the special valley to see, to feel the Presence of the Buddha.

Softly, calm the thoughts of excitement. Become a deep still pool to receive the blessing of the Buddha and then the Christ.

Within the stillness and the silence, be open to receive these gifts of your deep connection to the Lord of Light and the Lord of Love -- the Buddha and the Christ.

Stay in your focus. Stay in the quiet. Hold your spot in that sacred place at that sacred time and receive your blessing to be enveloped and then shared with the world as pure light and pure love.

Each person is different, a different container, but the joy -- being washed in Spirit -- the same. Let your mind go in peace.

We will all gather there in our hearts at the fullest point of the full moon.

Today, 5:42 p.m. New York time.

———————————

More from Margaret:

The Wesak gathering at the Full Moon of May 10 entwines the peoples of the world. It celebrates the gift of presence of the Buddha and His life and teaching.

With this linking of humanity, I am remembering when Buddhist monks from Tibet came to Rochester in July 1997, twenty years ago, to present the Buddhist teaching of the Kalachakra, The Cycle of Time.

In ancient times, this teaching would be given in public only four times per century. It was presented during intense times of turmoil and chaos when peace was needed. These teachings were given to the people to bring a state of unity, tranquility, understanding, and compassion. This would transform the individual to be a vehicle for establishing peace for society as a whole.

During part of the teaching, an elaborate sand mandala was constructed. At the end of the teaching, the sand mandala was dismantled and the sand was carried to a river and poured in the water to spread healing and blessings to the entire region.

I was present when the sand fell into the water, and it felt like a great burst of Light shot upwards. Powerful energy! This was amazing to behold.

The next day, the monks presented a land blessing to Ganondagan, a land sacred to the Seneca Nation of the Native American. The purpose was to spread healing energy and to honor the kinship and friendship of the Tibetans and Native Americans. I was present and I saw this great peace gathering.

The high healing and peace energy continued days afterwards. Days later, while driving through mountains, I look at the Sun and it begins dancing, spinning, flashing yellow, white, and red Light. A holy sight! This is etched into my memory. I feel the Sun was reflecting the power of the Holy Blessings given by the Tibetans.

This year at Wesak, when the world came together, I felt the same great expansive energy of Peace and Unity brought earlier by the Tibetan Buddhist monks.

Unification Festival

From Barbara:

We have just explained about the Wesak Festival that occurs at the full moon of Taurus. Before that, we told you about the Easter Festival. Well, here is one more spiritual festival, the Unification Festival, that we need to explain. It happens at the full moon of Gemini, June 9.

I think we have told you that every week we speak on television via PAX TV in Brazil. Carmen Balhestero, directress of a big spiritual center in Brazil, is in charge and we connect by speaking via computer SKYPE to television.

Carmen works closely with Saint Germain who channels to her continually. Recently, when Margaret and I were ready to speak on television, we heard Saint Germain speak in English to Carmen that June 9 will be the moment when strong Christ energy will come to the planet.

Was Saint Germain actually speaking to us so we would write it in the book for all to read? Would this help humanity unite itself so that will-to-good is dominant?

Often the personality of a human is dual. Also, nations are dual and many divide and oppose each other. The purpose of a Unification Festival is to help humanity focus on the will-to-good. The energies of the Christ will come in to help.

I ponder on why June 9 is chosen as the moment of the Unification Festival.

It is the full moon of Gemini. A full moon will increase water tides. The rising, movement of water.

I know much of the human body is water and so probably our body will react at the full moon on June 9. And so, it makes sense to me that the full moon on June 9 is being used for energies to come in to help change humans in a good way.

———————

From Margaret:

I want Emma Kunz to channel information for me about the Unification Festival. I say, dear Emma, we have just moved through the time of Easter at the full moon of Aries and Wesak at the time of the full moon of Taurus. Now we are facing the time of Unification at the full moon of Gemini on June 9, 9:09 a.m. What is the meaning of this special time period when the focus is on both ascension and unification? Can you comment?

Emma responds: Dear Margaret, within your question is the answer. Ascension comes when humanity is unified and each person is unified within the self as well as unified with all humanity.

You keep thinking of stones. They can be laying around in a haphazard manner or they can be assembled and made into a grand house.

Stones can be used to make walls to separate or to make pathways to walk in gardens and enjoy natural stone formations in Nature. Stones can be used to sit upon to bask in the view of a great valley. They can be stood upon to witness the power of the ocean waves below or to witness hot lava pools in a deep volcanic caldera.

Stones are the building blocks of earth.

One can throw stones or gather stones to create. Stones tell us the many histories on this planet.

When a person is unified within the self, there is no division. There is unity, harmony, and outreach. When there is peace within society, peace will reign on the planet.

People must look out for the good of the whole and for the good of each individual within the whole. This is Unification. When the individual is united with Nature and the life and joy of the Natural World, there is Oneness within All.

When one is merged with the Spiritual World, the Higher Worlds, where high ideals are set and projected to the human world, Peace will prevail on Earth.

This is Unification from the stones to humanity to the high loving beings who are way-showers -- the Christ, Buddha, other Holy Ones. All carry the frequency of Love and Light for the littlest to the grandest.

With understanding and when living this frequency without ego and with the heart focused, this is Ascension.

May the people ascend on June 9.

Come be with us.

Love,

Emma

—————————

From Barbara:

June 9, 9:09 a.m. we are ready at the Full Moon of Gemini to participate in the Unification Festival which will open even wider positive energies coming to the earth.

We softly play Soothing Relaxation Music.*

*See Glossary: Meditation music.

The Christ is with us. We feel him with us. We know He is with everyone who wants him at this time.

As we are listening to the music and meditating, the energies of the body feel smooth while taking in this special energy.

We know when we feel a high point. I am feeling a high point.

I take this energy and spread it throughout the world. I say to Mother Earth, I love you and I want to spread this high point of energy throughout you -- trees, birds, people, animals -- everything living on you.

I am excited that another thrust of powerful positive energy will be coming on August 7 at a Lunar Eclipse as well as on August 21, a Solar Eclipse which will be extremely powerful.

When we humans of this world join together during these auspicious moments, we can expect this will help Mother Earth and all on her.

I am not suggesting that all turmoil, negative energy, will immediately leave the Earth. But, it is my understanding that negative energy can be cleaned during these moments.

Perhaps turmoil can be considered as blessings in disguise because they appear when positive energy can remove them.

My thoughts will be on cleaning, sweeping, removing negative energy.

From Margaret:

June 9, 8:50 a.m.

For the Full Moon of Unification meditation on June 9, 9:09 am, I have in my mind the names of will-to-good people whose lives have been dedicated to Peace on Earth. Christ, Mary, Bawa Muhayaddean, Sai Baba, Master Goi, Buddha, Saint Germain. Then I add the names of other important people, Queen Noor, Jane Goodall, Mrs. Saionji, Mevlana, etc.

Also, I have in my mind others who raise peace energies of the planet -- professors of environmental research, doctors, educators, artists, musicians, etc.

From the Higher Worlds, I have received this message: *(You are thinking about) high frequency people -- souls lifting up the planet with high ideals and shining the Light of Love and creativity.*

Be like the lightning bug at every moment, show your Light. Show your Love. Embrace the world with the perfect frequency of Love.

All things grow with Love, the magic ingredient. It is priceless with no strings attached.

Radiance. Truth. Clarity. Generosity. Kindness. Compassion. Joy. Harmony.

Bask in these frequencies. Spread this Light. The trees hold this Light.

Within the branches of the trees, the psychic dolphins swim. They will come when Love calls. The world will come when Love calls.

Spin Love around the world. Take on the role of the Sun Disc. You are a Sun Disc to give and receive Light.

———————

Just before 9:09 a.m. the exact moment of the Full Moon, the Christ comes.

He says: Wake up, Margaret, I am here for everyone to join me this morning in the peace vibration for the planet. Rest, breathe, let your heart rejoice. The calmness has returned to the frequency of Mother Earth.

Balance, balance. Trees grow in perfect balance, straight up, equal on each side. Yet, on each branch, the rain falls equally, the sunlight shines equally.

Walk out. Follow me. I walk in the land of Love where everyone greets each other with an embrace of the heart.

It is very simple to be here. Place down the guarding ego and step out unencumbered. Everyone is equal in God's Love. Reflect that in your approach to life. It is very simple.

The infant comes to the planet with wonder and grace. Step back and greet each dawn as newborn, a new arrival to Mother Earth with her blessed animals, sea creatures, trees and mountains, sparkling water.

Bring this Love and joy to greet each creature on the planet whether a little bird singing or great trees waving in the wind or a new child just arriving or an old one leaving to begin a new life in another format. Continuation, continuation in balance and in Love.

Reach out. Reach inward. Reach all around with your Love. That is the only assignment for this day of Unification. Equal, Equal, Ascension.

AUM.

The Christ.

From Barbara:

10:04 a.m., message from the Higher World: *The crystals are all energized with the energy of Christ.*

I have held my Herkimer crystals in my hands during the whole meditation and I am told: *Everything is crystal. Conceive of everything being a crystal.*

More from Margaret:

I ask my crystals to comment on the meditation we have just experienced.

I receive: Dear Margaret, the meditation is for the unification of all worlds -- the Crystal World, the Human World, the Natural World, the Higher Worlds. This is the moment of Unification.

Everything is crystal. Everything is Light. Everything is powered by Love.

Through the concepts of universality and unification comes Peace. Peace on the planet. The humans are on board! This is the Moment of Ascension!

CHAPTER 6

Earth Day, May Day

Earth Day

From Barbara:

Today is April 22, which some call Earth Day, and the minds of thousands of people are on the dilemma of climate change. They do not understand. They are marching to support scientists who are looking into the reality of climate change. Many have gone to Washington, D.C., the nation's capital, to march for science. We understand that 600 cities around the world are experiencing marches.

———————

From Margaret:

I ask Emma to comment:

Emma: It is exciting to see the people mobilized to support science and the environment on Earth Day.

Look at the uneven weather patterns this spring. Very warm, very cold, thirty-six inches of snow at one time. Unevenness.

Margaret, in your growing up time, the seasons moved in progression in an even way. They were separate and distinct. Now the weather is more extreme with fierce thunderstorms, tornadoes, droughts, fires and floods spreading throughout the country and the world.

There is so much rain in upstate New York that Lake Ontario residents need to use sandbags to keep the water off driveways, lawns, and roads. Soon, the houses will be affected. This flooding occurs on the Great Lakes that do not have tides like the oceans.

The beaches of the East Coast of the United States are eroded away yearly by high winds and storm surges. Delaware, Maryland and New Jersey communities need to replenish sand so summer vacationers can go to the shores.

The North Pole has lost its ice. Greenland has lost its snow. The oceans are rising and the rising temperatures affect the sea and coral life. This has taken place within your lifetime. When going to the beach in North Carolina in the 1950's, there were three distinct zones of different sands to reach the water -- very soft sand, moderately soft sand and very hard sand at the water's edge. Now there is hardly any beach -- just the dunes and houses -- no broad expanse of beach.

Earthquakes, volcanoes, magma rising -- the earth's surface is changing.

Climate change, environmental change, are on everyone's doorstep. Think about what you have observed over what you have seen and experienced in a lifetime.

In the last four years, you have experienced the Polar Vortex coming south from the North Pole. Niagara Falls froze. This year a windstorm in early March blew the shingles off your garage roof. I think you can call this a change in the climate.

My Blessings and Love,

Emma

Barbara Wolf; Margaret Anderson

From Barbara;

Earth's heat has intensified because of the sun, which is much brighter than before and it is hotter.

Why, I ask myself.

Also, storms are not moderate, and there are earthquakes in Japan, drought in Africa. Will the Earth shift? Is the Earth in danger?
————————

From Margret:

I channel again, asking for the cause of the acceleration of change, and here is what I received.

Yes, the sun is 1,000 times more intense with solar storms, etc. Before this, the sun was bland. You could stare at it and not be affected. Now you can hardly look directly at it.

The interior of the earth is heating up. Time has changed in relationship to dimensional changes. The days feel shorter. Time can be expanded when needed.

To have a moderate climate, the planet needs moderation among its inhabitants.

Humanity, with its overpopulation and its insatiable consumption of goods, has affected the environment. The elements of air, water, and land have been damaged by human pollution.

More and more, the people of the world are turning to the wisdom of Native Americans and other indigenous elders of the world who have lived in harmony with Nature for thousands and thousands of years.

Making a difference will be the giving of love, respect, sharing, honoring, being thankful, giving Light and healing.

If the energy fields are stable, then the environment will be stable. Also, the land is affected in a positive manner by humanity praying, meditating, chanting, singing in harmony. This is called living in grace.

All systems communicate -- cells, plants, trees, animals, stones, crystals. It is time for the human to stop shouting and stomping and making loud noises. Let them follow the example of the people gathering continually at the World Peace Sanctuary at Mount Fuji where everyone prays for peace on Earth and harmony with Nature.

Humanity should follow the bright words of the lovely video, Feel Love and Peace by Mieko Sakai.*

*See: Glossary: Feel, Love and Peace.

If everyone played this video and followed the mindful Love sequence, there would be indeed a change for the good on our planetary systems. Human relations would change for the better. There would be Peace on Earth.

From Barbara:

Some call today Earth Day, and others do not. In any case, however one uses the name, the day brings positive energies to Mother Earth who is just now experiencing negativity.

Some are marching today in Washington, D. C. for science, and our sympathies are with them. We will work today at Mendon Ponds Park, the eastern powerful energy point of the Niagara Escarpment. From here, we will send out powerful positive energy to stimulate the positive energy being sent out to the world. Here is the background.

Millions of years ago, this area was a big sea. This was during the time when no negativity existed on Mother Earth. When sea life living in the big sea died, their shells fell and collected with other shed shells. Eventually, the collection of shells, together with rocks, etc. grew into mountains.

Today, the sea is gone and the big expanse of positive energy mountains is called the Niagara Escarpment.

Yes, Margaret and I want to use this positive energy to help Mother Earth who, at this moment is experiencing much negativity. We will drive to Mendon Ponds.

The day is bright and sunny as we are driving to Mendon Ponds. When we arrive, we park near the water, and on the car radio we listen to beautiful music as we begin to meditate.

And yes, we do send energy around the world to support Science for the people.

Here is something I find interesting. I have just learned that a recent article in the Journal of Science explains a scientific method of bringing water to the desert. A device the size of a tissue box can extract daily water from desert air!

What a FANTASTIC discovery! This morning we are happy, happy, happy as we drive to Mendon Ponds Park to meditate and send positive energy to Science.

In the water near us, we see two geese. Mates, we think. It is spring and the females are either already sitting on eggs to hatch baby geese or they will soon sit on eggs.

A couple days ago, when we were at Lamberton Conservatory, we asked where is the tame female duck, and we are told she is sitting on eggs somewhere in the conservatory. But, we are told, to date, her nest has not been found. Earlier, they had found her sitting on a nest of eggs, and they removed the eggs because the female duck had not been fertilized. Therefore, the eggs cannot hatch.

In any case, today we see at Mendon Ponds two geese together and we feel these are mates and there will be eggs turning into babies. We send the geese and all of Nature positive energies.

When we leave Mendon Ponds, we drive less than two miles to visit Wild Wings, a permanent refuge for injured birds. Next to the parking lot we see two grazing horses. One of them, a big beautiful white horse, is close to us and we spend a bit of time looking at him -- sending positive energy to both horses and to the Animal Kingdom.

When we enter the Wild Wings bird refuge, we walk slowly along the homes of the birds, looking at them as they look at us.

We send them Love, and one bird hoots at us. We return his hoot.

It is wonderful being here in this tranquil place of birds!

———————————

From Margaret:

In the early morning, before going to Mendon Ponds, I walk around the local reservoir. The day begins very fresh and the walkers here are joyful for the bright spring morning. Dogs of all sizes are happy to be out walking with their families. I find such pleasure in greeting each person with a smile or a comment to have a beautiful day. I stop to talk with each puppy. The littlest are the most enthusiastic, but all the dogs love to greet someone who loves them.

I carry bouncing dog energy when I return to the car and we drive to Mendon Ponds. Here, I feel the intense positive energies of the harmony of the environment. This is augmented by the flowering trees, the high beauty of April. The trees and plants are greeting the spring in all their power and glory. Mother Earth is wearing her greatest finery.

At Mendon Ponds, we begin meditating and we are soon submerged in the power of the Niagara Escarpment. We send this power to the entire world. It feels as if we are swimming in a great ocean of Light.

When it is time to leave this glorious place, we drive to Wild Wings* to see injured members of the Bird Kingdom.

*See Glossary: Wild Wings.

Volunteer Judge John Ninfo takes these birds with staff members to show them to inner city school children so they can see the power and grace of these birds. I feel the strength and wonder of the birds is transferred to the children.

Before entering Wild Wings, we enter and greet two beautiful grazing horses enjoying new grass. We send our love to them and to the Horse World.

As we enter the Wild Wings enclosure to greet the birds, we see them basking in the warm morning sunlight. A beautiful red-tailed hawk is spreading her wings to receive the warmth of the sun's powerful light. A true sunbath.

Like an earlier visit, we phone our Native American friend SilverStar so she can hear an owl calling *Hoot Hoooo....Hoot Hooooo.* We have been told that birds are telepathic messengers who can send out to the birds of the world the sacred message of peace, harmony and unity.

It is fun greeting all the birds -- the large bald eagle, golden eagle, turkey vulture, red-tailed hawk, barn owl, and little screech owls.

The bobcat here who was raised as a pet and cannot go into the wild, greets us as she relaxes in the sun.

This has been a magic day!

May Day

From Barbara:

May 1, called May Day, has a special meaning for me. I think of it as the end of cold weather and the beginning of spring which is a relief after a hard winter.

When I was a child, on May Day my three sisters and I would create small bouquets of flowers to put them on the doorsteps of friends and neighbors.

After my formal education was completed, I moved to Europe where I lived for a time in Spain. May Day festivities were held, and it was fun attending celebrations where people sang around a decorated tree or sculpture. Today, Spain has a competition tradition of selecting the May Day best sculptures and songs.

May Day is celebrated in Germany with bonfires at night and dancing around a maypole. This pole is usually a tree covered with streamers.

In Greece, May Day is celebrated in some areas by flower wreathes placed on doors of houses and apartments and even on balconies.

Parades are held in Poland to observe May 1 as a state holiday.

In Canada, the city of Toronto celebrates May Day by concentrating on dancing called the Morris Dance. This is a legacy from Great Britain where this dance is performed around a maypole. The crowning of a May Queen is a tradition continuing from the far past.

I know that at least half the world will have fun on May Day. I am happy because spring is here and Nature is in full bloom. The sun is shining brightly. The day is warm. Yes, I am happy.

CHAPTER 7

Herkimer, Howe Caverns, Concord

F rom Barbara:

It is the end of May and, yes, summer is on our doorstep.

Margaret and I are driving to Concord, Massachusetts to honor distinguished Bill Andrews, who has just died.

Concord, Massachusetts is far from us, and so we make our drive a two-day event. We leave early in the morning to reach our first stop about two hours away, at the Sun Disc area of Herkimer. Sun Discs are the source of great Light for this planet. Herkimer is also the residence of quartz diamonds born here around 500 million years ago.

When we begin our journey, we know rain has been forecast, but we wish to be optimistic. And so we have our minds on sunshine. Well, a suggestion of rain is with us when we begin, and at first it is slight, but then it increases.

I say to the sun, "HELLO, SUNSHINE. WE NEED YOU!!!" After a few minutes, the rain eases although it does not entirely stop.

The road is fast because it is the New York State Thruway and there is little early morning traffic. We go along without incident, and before noon, we reach the powerful Sun Disc Light area at Herkimer. We are in one of the three most powerful Sun Disc areas in North America. The other two are Pinnacle Mountain in Arkansas and Denali in Alaska.

When we arrive at Herkimer, few visitors are here, and we think there will be many, many by mid afternoon. Digging for Herkimer quartz diamonds is a joyous event for diggers. Since we are reaching the holiday Memorial Day weekend when many will not be working, we think this place will soon see many diggers with buckets and equipment ready to search for the powerful crystals. Whatever they find, they can keep.

Yes, it is wonderful being here again. We don't come often, but every time is wonderful. We enter the big crystal store with its hundreds of crystals looking at us and we looking at them. WOW!!! Such a FANTASTIC site!

Behind one long, long crystal counter is a man we recognize from earlier visits, and we speak briefly with him as our eyes roam the displays. Of course we want to take all the crystals home with us! Well, next time.

Now we climb stairs to reach the second floor where Randy is waiting for us.

Who is Randy?

An ancient, petrified being recently found off the African island country called Madagascar. He is alone up here. There are no other ancient ones living in the store, but he is among hundreds and hundreds of ancient quartz Herkimer diamond crystals.

Actually, we only see Randy's petrified head. That is all that has been discovered off the coast of Madagascar. To my knowledge, throughout the world there have been found only two ancient beings similar to Randy.

I have a fascination for ancient beings, such as dinosaurs estimated to have begun living on the earth between 231 and 243 million years ago.

Of course we all know that they have been extinct a very long time. However, what fascinates me is that recently scientists have decided that some birds today are descendants of these ancient beings!

I have not read anywhere about these birds, but a search of the Internet brings me information.

To visit ancient beings, I have visited the Rochester Museum & Science Center that displays two skeletons aged between 65 to 100 million years. They are the remains of what once lived in the Rochester, New York area. Apparently, a number of skeletons have been unearthed in the Rochester area which seemed to have been an ideal place for ancient ones to live.

At the museum, visitors are allowed to touch a real ancient bone. I touched one, and I was allowed to rest my hand on this bone for a long time. Can you imagine touching a bone that is between 65 and 100 million years old?!!!

Next door to this museum is the Strasenburgh Planetarium where I watched a video on ancient beings. The video was very 'real life'. I sat in the dark exhibit area and watched fierce dinosaurs suddenly appear in front of me. Their roar was VIOLENT! Their action of fierceness was REAL LIFE!

In fact, the video was so 'real life', the audience was warned before it began that young children could be scared. Well, I did not have to be a young child to be affected by what was happening. My thought was that I am lucky to be watching rather than actually being attacked!

––––––––––––––––

Now, let us return to thinking about Randy who is living on the second floor of the Herkimer diamond store. We say good-bye to him and we climb down the stairs saying good-bye to all the crystals in the store and we are soon on our way to Howe Caverns. Nearby, we intend to stay a night in a motel, if we can find accommodations.

When we arrive at Howe Caverns, we find cars filling to capacity a large parking lot! Apparently, Howe Caverns is second only to Niagara Falls for being the most popular nature attraction in New York State. In the main entrance building, we encounter many tourists waiting for the next tour to begin.

Several years ago, when we visited Howe Caverns, we encountered busloads of young children screaming and running around without discipline and with no regard for what was there for their minds to ingest. We could not stay.

Last year, when we visited the Herkimer diamond crystals, we had no intention of also visiting the Howe Caverns. But, when we were looking at the crystals at Herkimer, the entities living at the Howe Caverns suddenly, in telepathy, asked us to visit them after leaving Herkimer.

Well, our schedule was too tight for that, and we did not visit them. But, this year we have come to visit them.

We find a hotel is at the edge of the Howe Caverns property and we stop to ask if there would be overnight accommodations for us.

YES. And so, we have ordered accommodations.

We know we do not have to be physically in the caverns to be with the entities living there. They are not physical beings. In the night, in sleep time, we can be with them.

Now we learn something unusual. At 5 p.m., the motel office closes and everyone working there leaves. No one will be available to attend to our requests except a man not living at the motel who can be phoned and he will come to help.

Whoever heard of a motel operating with no one in charge?

As for us, we like this. Yes. PERFECT.

And so, we have stayed the night. And yes, in the morning we are happy with our overnight visit with the entities. How long have these entities been associated with the Howe Caverns? At least 500,000 years.

———————

In the morning we turn our attention to driving to Concord, Massachusetts to Bill Andrew's funeral gathering.

As we leave the Howe Caverns, we are quickly in a mountainous area that is heavily carpeted with green trees and there is a softness to these mountains. We question ourselves whether or not we are correct when we think these mountains may have been at one time connected to Scotland and its soft vibrations. The connection, if correct, would be millions of years ago.

And yes, we learn there is a linkage between Scotland and North America in prehistoric times.

Our map shows us we are just south of the Appalachian Mountains, and we know there is a trail called Appalachian Trail beginning far south and running far north. We have a friend who walks the trail nearly every summer, and he says it takes a long time to walk. While walking, he begins feeling like Nature.

Well, we may not feel like Nature as we are driving along, but we have a strong feeling of Mother Earth's Nature here.

Now it is Margaret's time to talk about the journey.

———————

From Margaret:

Before we leave on our journey, I receive a channeling from the crystals.

They speak aspects of their force field:

Light Energy, a gift to Mother Earth. Peace Radiance. Sound and Light. Receivers and broadcasters.

Hello, Margaret, we are at your service.

We are your friends from below ground -- Herkimers, the Howe Caverns crystals, and the sticky stones that hold the diamonds.

The diamonds embrace/encase the energy field of the Herkimer Sun Disc which energizes and balances Mother Earth's energy field -- frequencies that bring Light and life to the life forms on the planet.

Sun power brings healing and vitality to the entire Solar System and beyond. The Sun Disc at Herkimer holds and augments that power and directs where it should go.

The Sun Disc sends only positive frequencies/vibrations. It is the feeling of dawn at every moment -- that particular time, that particular power.

Polish your thoughts to receive and give out Light. If you are cloudy with upset thoughts, you cannot fully receive our joyful gift of Light, healing, and growth.

Crystals record events and sing their own songs. The Herkimers are clear Light, focused on constant power going outwards for strengthening, clearing, enhancing life on Mother Earth's surface and beneath. Our Light shines universally. That is why people are drawn to our presence.

New York State Herkimer crystals and the Arkansas Crystal Vortex have been your focus this morning, and rightly so. Combine that with the powerful Niagara Escarpment to lift the frequency of the continent.

Power Points, Power Places, Resonated in the heart frequency -- let the crystals work their mastery of growing and enhancing life in a balanced way of peace and harmony.

Barbara Wolf; Margaret Anderson

Margaret, you have just had a crystal bath this morning.

With love from your neighbors, the crystals, allies, friends of Mother Earth and her soil and water.

Smile and you will shine like us. The greatest armor is a true smile.

Dear Crystal friends, I say, you are more flexible than I.

They respond, yes, we know.

I say, thank you for being here.

They respond, thank you for being here. We meet at this time to work for Mother Earth -- not to decorate a room. Crystal humor.

Stay in our Light and you will be at peace. If the people of the world could harmonize with the crystals, there will be peace on Earth.

To receive and give Light, to receive and give Peace, to receive and give Love.

Peace, Love, and Light.

More from Margaret:

The crystal channeling message has been given to me before leaving for Concord, Massachusetts to honor Bill Andrews. First there is a stop in Herkimer and then a stop at Howe Caverns.

We begin our long journey at 7:00 a.m. and at first the traffic is light. However, when we reach the New York State Thruway, heavy trucks begin moving fast, some over sixty-five miles per hour. This makes us nervous so we begin playing classical music on the car radio to counter heavy truck traffic movement plus rain and fog.

However, when we reach pleasant rolling hills and then mountains, we relax and begin feeling the friendliness of the approaching foothills of the Adirondacks.

Also, I begin feeling the radiance of the Sun Disc at Herkimer before we arrive. I think we have a long way to go, but, to my surprise, we are just a mile and a half before reaching Herkimer.

I need to mention that along the way, we see deep cuts in the earth to make a passageway for the interstate highway and local roads. Here, we see the layers of deposits of the Niagara Escarpment that were formed approximately 450 million years ago.

When we reach the grounds of the Herkimer diamond mines, we find many students on bus tours who are probably ready to dig for crystals. We know that Herkimer crystals may be 500 million years old.*

* See Glossary: Herkimer Diamond Crystals.

We stop and enter a large 1880 converted barn structure called the Herkimer Diamond Mine Gem - Mineral Shop, Museum. This building houses the crystal shop on the first floor and the museum of crystals and fossils on the second floor.

Upstairs, Barbara is especially interested in an ancient fossil from Madagascar called Randy. I prefer looking at crystal displays and especially the one that has a large crystal bed from Arkansas. This was probably part of the ancient Atlantean crystal beds.

Then, close to Randy, I see a small Herkimer crystal bed with tiny crystals and one crystal is growing much larger than the others. This is amazing. It shows that each crystal grows in its own time.

Some crystals grow in cluster beds, and others are separate. Can some of the separate ones be implants? I love thinking that perhaps some Herkimer crystals are from off-world, a gift to Mother Earth.

When we leave the Herkimer diamond crystal building, I sit outside and channel more. I have my Herkimer crystals with me and I am thinking they are with their brothers and sisters.

Here is their channeling:

We have all come home to begin to start again. Each one holds the resonance/frequency of the moment of its birth -- the time, the place, the creative environment. To be of the Earth and yet separate. That is the delight of the crystals.

Some crystals stay as a family unit welded together in structure. Others, double pointed, stand alone or have been removed from their earlier place of attachment. All hold Light. All are here to augment Life on the planet.

Through song, the crystals broadcast hope for the future. They have reached their awareness long before humans can catch them. We are out there -- around the bend -- in other dimensions.

You have to smooth out your frequencies to get on our frequency. Non-attachment. To operate on the frequency of Love and Light. No baggage.

No agenda. Just presence.

Try to be like us. Be in your complete state of perfection. In that state, you can communicate with trees, stones, boulders, crystals. You can travel through the layers of caverns -- the interiors of mountains.

(We are) apartment dwellers living down and down and down and down. So many layers of Life. Cherish what is seen and unseen.

You honored the green growing spruce tree with light green growth.

Hello, dear Spruce Tree with the delicate new fingers, candles, growth extensions of many years.

You are traveling at the New Moon of the Tree, May 25, the Spiritual Law of Equality.* All the same. All are One. All are Equal in validity.

*See Glossary: Symbols and Calendar.

Machines work in harmony when all parts function equally. Societies prosper when all work in harmony -- when parts are equal and function equally.

Equal gift. Equal Life. Equal Love. Equal Light.

I ask, can one outshine a crystal?

You have to be a crystal to shine like a crystal -- clarity, truth and love.

We are Earth Guardians.

I return to the car to get out the Blessings Chimes to ring for all the crystals.

Then we head toward the Howe Caverns, driving through exquisite rolling fields and steep hills and valleys with great peace energy.

At Howe Caverns, we stay overnight at the Howe Caverns Motel within the energy field of the crystals.

In the evening I receive a channeling from the Howe Caverns entities:

The quiet time has descended and the day's activity has slowly ceased. The electronic noise has diminished and the sound of the Earth at Peace is once again. This is when we, the entities of Howe Caverns and all the caves and underworld passages, can relax, take a breath, and communicate with like-frequency beings. We respond to heart-felt greetings in the rhythm of Mother Earth's beings. We are close to her heartbeat and can feel all her thoughts and wishes and distress.

The great Mother Earth has the generosity to allow and to support the homes of many species of life forms. The humans need to honor this gift she has given. Rushing, cutting, drilling, building on or near the surface causes her great pain. Treat her body, her elements, as you would treat your body.

Honor clean water, clean air, pristine land.

Tap into Mother Earth's sounding -- her heartbeat -- her breath (the winds), her song (the sea and the waves), and the chorus of the birds at dawn. Listen to the music of the leaves rustling, the water flowing in a stream, the crickets, the frogs, the cicadas, the squirrels, the flight hum of the hummingbird.

We are below ground, but we hear them -- the Sounds of Nature. Above ground, do you hear them when the mind and busy-ness are in a hurry? Peace time is the time to unwind.

Listen to the Stars crackle; listen to the Sun's approach at dawn; sink into the Love of Mother Earth.

We are the Entities, the beings at Howe Caverns and the underworld of the Planet.

The next day, at dawn, I sketch the beautiful sunrise over the valley and the mountain across the way. The sunrise highlights the mountain.

At 7:30 a.m. we are on the road driving toward Massachusetts. Our thoughts are on circumventing the big city of Albany to reach the Massachusetts Turnpike, and yes, we do.

At the beginning of this morning's trip, the sun is shining on water falling, streaming down rock layers. These rocks are the grand walls of the Niagara Escarpment cut out for the highway. I love seeing water running, cascading down in delicate trickles caught by the sunlight and made into a sheen of mirrors.

The rocks speak: *We are the encyclopedia of Mother Earth's history,*

_____

When we cross the Hudson River, which we have so often crossed by train, we cheer that we are making good progress.

Now we reach the Taconic Volcanic Mountains which we know little about. 440 million years ago these ancient mountains were once volcanic islands that collided with the continent to form a tall mountain range.*

*See Glossary: Taconic Mountains.

Massive rock layers that have been thrust up. White, black and red-brown rock layers, solid and thick. This introduces us to the powerful frequency that welcomes us to Massachusetts State.

The highway is tree lined, beautiful, with the new growth of leaves. The sun is out to rejoice in the day.

When we reach Concord, we make our way to the Marriott Residence Inn where we will stay. We contact Barbara's sister, Shirley, and we are soon at a dinner gathering with their family to honor Shirley's husband, Bill.

_____

From Barbara:

My dear brother-in-law, Bill Andrews was close to 90 years old when he died very quickly without suffering. His time was up.

Bill was a good man, always positive. A retired professor at Harvard Law. An accomplished piano player who to the end played magnificent music. We listened to him playing a few weeks ago when we were in

in Tucson, Arizona with him and my sister.

_____

From Barbara and Margaret:

May 28:

We go to Sleepy Hollow Cemetery for Bill's funeral service. At his gravesite, we see two navy personnel standing at attention, honoring Bill's former service in the military. When the funeral service ends, they will play taps and present an American flag to Shirley.

Before the service begins, we wait for others to arrive. They will be walking through the woods following a bagpiper. When they are close, we begin hearing the sounds of the bagpipe.

As we wait, we look at turtles in a large pond lying on logs to receive the warmth of the sun on their glistening backs. As we watch, we listen to birds -- woodpeckers, the cardinals, etc. Squirrels are dashing about.

As we are listening to the birds and watching the squirrels run about, the bagpipe is louder and louder, announcing the arrival of the walkers ready to honor Bill Andrew's life. A squirrel moves to an over-hanging high branch to have a good view. Our hearts are moved.

When the service begins, it is organized in a relaxed, organized and loving way. We all loved Bill and we are sad he is not with us. We hope he will know from his perch in the Higher Worlds that we are here at his gravesite, honoring him.

The next day we return to New York State.

CHAPTER 8

Alaska

From Barbara:

This year I will not be in Alaska during the Summer Solstice. However, I have visited Alaska several times, and June 1991 I was there at the time of the Summer Solstice, June 21, 1991. Wow! It was 68 degrees and people were walking around minus shirtsleeves. For them, the weather was hot.

Let me tell you a bit about being in Alaska in 1991.

Specifically, I wanted to be in Barrow, Alaska, at the Bering Straights, and I was there! It is a place where the sun begins to think about not going to bed for the night. I was close to the North Pole. I am told that the longest night lasts for 67 days.

In 1991, I never heard a word about drought. Now, in 2017, I hear a lot about Alaskan drought. Places like Anchorage and Fairbanks are far below normal when it comes to a normal amount of snow on the ground. As for icebergs, too many have disappeared and many more are on the way to disappearing.

It is my understanding that polar bears live on icebergs from which they hunt seals for food, their preferred food. In 1991, I remember standing in front of a huge windowless barn that did not seem to be connected to a farm. I asked myself, where is the farm equipment -- tractors, etc.? Something seemed abnormal. Then I was told that this huge windowless barn was for polar bears. When a polar bear, for one reason or another, decided to spend a lot of time on land rather than on icebergs, this became a problem for whoever was living in the area. The polar bears would forage for food in the populated areas rather than hunt offshore for seals.

And so the roaming land polar bears were captured and put in the barn and routinely fed until weather permitted them to be put on the ice. I assume they were probably transported a distance from the barn.

Today, because of loss of ice around Alaska, I think there are many land-roaming polar bears lacking icebergs for their homes. Probably homelessness has become a problem for them, and I have even heard that polar bears can be facing possible extinction if the northern part of Mother Earth is not returned to its former state of being.

Just now I am also worried about Denali which is near the center of the landmass of Alaska. It has recently received a 5.2 earthquake which means Mother Earth is rumbling.

This indicates imbalance.

As mentioned earlier, Denali is one of three major Sun Discs for North America. The other two are Pinnacle Mountain in Arkansas and Herkimer in New York.

From Margaret:

We need to immediately spread peace/harmony energies to Denali because earthquakes usually mean imbalance. We do not want imbalance in such an important area as Denali, a Sun Disc location.

We also need to give positive energy to the North Pole to help the balance of Mother Earth. We begin meditating for both Denali and the North Pole when Barbara remarks that the control entities at the Roslyn Chapel Sun Disc are here with us. She also says Roslyn Chapel is the most major Sun Disc for the entire world.

I ask why these entities are here and why they make themselves known to Barbara.

They answer: We are here to give support to your work. The world crystals are aware -- your Citrines (from Brazil) and your Herkimer crystals have called us.

The Sun Discs help regulate the Crystalline Grid which influences the shift of the planet. As the Dolphins said, to work with the crystals helps bring balance.

We guard and unfold the energy of the Sun Disc.

Barbara is attuned to us.

You are attuned to Pinnacle.

ALL SUN DISCS ARE INVOLVED.

There needs to be a uniting force field -- all Sun Discs raise the energy on the planet. Not just one. All. All stand up at the same time. All work together at the same time.

(Margaret) you hold many Sun Disc energies in your energy field – Shasta, Lake O'Hara/Lake Louise, Pinnacle Mountain, Galveston, Asheville, Herkimer, Hawaii.

Remember this -- the blanket concept -- the unity concept -- the whole activated.

We are here now because of the uncertainty of the times. All of humanity world wide is on edge. People are calling out for help, for stability and right action. We hear the calls. We come to address this issue.

The mountains hold the stability of the Earth. Set your vibration with the mountains. They give strength. They give balance.

The crystals give strength and give balance. Work in a united field on the crystalline base through any door to Mother Earth's heart.

We are here.

With love from your friends of other worlds -- Sun Disc live vibration.

––––––––––––

After the channeling, Barbara and I coordinate to begin our meditation again. This time we are listening to the soft music of Saint Germain.

I have with me my crystals -- three golden Citrine crystals from Brazil, three Herkimer Diamond crystals, and one black Obsidian from Mount Shasta. Each is associated with a Sun Disc. (There are 144 Sun Discs throughout the world.)

I can feel immediately that I am in the crystal rooms of the Chugach Mountains. These mountains are within viewing range of Anchorage. On an earlier trip to Alaska, we first learned about them as we were viewing them from a hotel in the outskirts of Anchorage. At that time, we learn in meditation how to visit these powerful crystal rooms.

Today, in meditation, I go to these crystal rooms to gather up Peace, Love and Light energies which I immediately send to Denali. Then I also send this energy to the North Pole. I know Barbara is doing the same.

––––––––––––

Suddenly I look up and there above me are two Angels flying with scrolls that have the words May Peace Prevail On Earth and Peace, Love and Light.

I ask them to fly over the Sun Discs of North America and also over all the other Sun Discs of the world. As a final comment, I want to say that all the Sun Discs are connected with each other. The energy of today's work will be connected to all the Sun Discs.

May Peace Prevail On Earth. Peace, Love and Light.

From Barbara:

When I visited Alaska in 1991, I had a wonderful time. I took a lot of photographs and I wrote extensive notes on the trip. My thought now is to add here some of the notes for you. I think you may enjoy them.

Here is the first note for you. I am on a plane flying from Anchorage to the city of Nome and, as we are flying, I am looking down at snow-capped mountains. They are magnificent!

These mountains remind me of Tibet, and I am remembering that I was in Tibet a year before going to Alaska. I feel the vibrations here are so similar to Tibet!

I think the Tibetans would fit in well with the Alaskan Eskimos. They have the same happy mannerisms. Big smiles.

I am looking out of the plane window and I am seeing that now there are clouds over the mountains and so I am only seeing the tops. Mount McKinley, the White Man's name for Denali, is in the distance.

Now the pilot is telling us that this is the tallest mountain in the world. More than 22,000 feet from the base. He says other mountains might begin at higher altitudes than Denali, but they are not as tall.

And then the clouds close in and we are flying along seeing little until just before Nome where we will be landing. The weather clears and we are looking down at Norton Sound, the part of the Bering Sea near Nome.

I see big pieces of ice floating on Norton Sound. Big pieces floating everywhere except near the shore.

The land at the Sound is flattish, barren, without trees. Snow here and there dotting the landscape.

The pilot lands us at Nome Airport to discharge some passengers and pick up other others. I remain on board. When all is ready, he takes us into the air, and we are heading north toward Kotzebue. In a few minutes, he tells us, we will be crossing the Arctic Circle. And he adds that above the Circle, the sun will not set at these longest days of the year. It is the time of the Summer Solstice here.

He says the sun will circle across the sky, and at Kotzebue, where we are headed, the sun will disappear briefly behind horizon-based mountains. But the sun will not go down at the horizon for two weeks. Then it will set only very briefly. In the winter, there are one and one-half hours of sunlight and no sunshine. Just light.

When we land at Kotzebue, we are told the temperature is eighty-three degrees! In the 1950's, there was a record of eighty-five degrees.

Well, we landing passengers are feeling that it is hotter than eighty-three degrees! We are all suffering from wearing too many clothes.

I have lunch in Kotzebue at the Nullagvik Hotel, and from the dining room, I have a good view of the beach and the Bering Sea. I am told this part of the Bering Sea is called the Kotzebue Sound, and I learn that the Bering Sea goes into the Arctic Ocean.

After lunch, I go to the NANA Museum to attend a sound and light show explaining Arctic animals. And then I see Eskimos storytelling and dancing accompanied by drums. The drums are played by elderly men and women and the dancing is by teen-aged or a bit older youth.

We 'watchers' are invited to join in the dancing and the female dancers teach me and other women how to dance properly while the male dancers are teaching the invited males how to dance. The female and male movements are different in that the male movements are more forceful.

———————

Now I want to tell you that during the month of March, Alaska has a dogsled race called the Iditarod. It begins in Anchorage and ends in

Nome. I was not in Alaska during the month of March, but I certainly heard many stories about the Iditarod.

In 1991, I was on a bus going to meet a man named Howard who raced in the Iditarod. Soon I learned that this bus ride to meet him would be different from the usual bus ride. As if we were participating in an Iditarod, we would race Howard and his dogs to the meeting place.

I looked out of a bus window at Howard and his dogs waiting on a nearby pathway. The dogs, tongues hanging out, were waiting impatiently for the race to begin.

And yes, it did begin, and I continued looking out the window at Howard and his dogs. We went along a bit and then the terrain changed from flat to a bit hilly. Will this hill beat the dogs trying to win?

No.

The bus driver slowed a bit, and then a bit more as the dogs struggled to overcome the hill.

And yes, they did.

Within minutes, they had reached the end of the race and they had won!

The bus driver stopped the bus and we climbed out and went to the still-harnessed dogs lying down, tongues panting. Their eyes showed success! They had won!

The eyes of Howard waiting beside his dogs also showed success.

While speaking to Howard, we learned that one dog had earlier saved his life and all the other dogs. They started crossing an iced waterway and all had just left the shore when the ice broke. Immediately, without command, the lead dog turned around and brought the dog team to shore, including Howard.

Howard told us that last spring the Iditarod competition happened during an intense storm that forced the dog teams to run blind for nearly fifteen hours. They had to feel with their feet where to run. If the snow felt packed, then they knew it was packed by race people before the race. If the snow was soft, they knew they were off the path and could get lost. The storm was so fierce, and the temperature was so cold, they knew the consequences would have been awful if the contenders got lost.

While in Nome, I learned about the great gold rush that brought as many as 40,000 to Nome to pan for gold. They were spread out for miles and miles along the beach, and there were so many panning for gold, a claim site consisted of the length of a shovel on either side of where one was standing. If anyone left the site for any reason, it was immediately taken by another gold seeker.

Gold Fever was the term used to describe the desperate ones coming from all over the world to become rich.

Well, folks, writing to you here has brought back great memories. I loved Alaska. I still love Alaska.

From Margaret:

My first visit to Alaska was in mid-March 2013, the second anniversary of the disastrous earthquake in Japan, March 11, 2011. We were alerted by the Higher Worlds that there could be a possible large earthquake at any moment in Alaska and we are to prevent this by going to Anchorage to put down the smooth energies of love and harmony.

We fly over the great mountains of Alaska, seeing the expanse of the glaciers. I think of frozen water and I see the water crystals on the plane's window. I give Love to the water crystals, and then to all the glaciers, and then to all the snow of Alaska. A blanket of Love to calm, to settle the land.

We arrive in Anchorage and the next morning we take a cab to a boat launch point that is snow-covered. The sun is shining but it is only 13 degrees Fahrenheit.

I find a place to carve into the crusty snow rows of twenty-two Vortex Symbols to stabilize the land frequency. I draw each Symbol and encircle it while speaking the name. When all the Symbols are drawn and encircled, I speak to the mountains, the snow, and the water that the Vortexes have been put down. A magpie sits on a nearby post observing me.

When I finish, I see the morning sunlight shining on the Symbols. The snow seems brighter. My fingers are cold, but my feet and body are warm.

Throughout the planting of the Symbols, Barbara sends out many OMs.

But it is too cold to linger and the cab driver is waiting. In fact, he is relieved at what we are doing. He is Egyptian and has felt a deep sense of dread that an earthquake would happen. Yes, he knows what we are doing and he says he is glad we have come.

———————

Now, this same Egyptian taxi driver takes us to the zoo to greet the Animal Kingdom. When we arrive, we buy our tickets and begin walking on a snow/ice pathway sprinkled with tiny black particles that are either rock or ash chips. These particles keep our feet steady and we walk with our minds on the animals rather than on our feet.

The entrance booth has given us a map of the zoo and we head first to the polar bear compound. This zoo is unlike any zoo we have visited. All the animals seem to be outside even though the temperature drops significantly during the winter. It is 11 degrees when we are here and we are dressed warm enough to stand this temperature, but our toes feel cold.

Two polar bears, one male and one female, are parading around their large enclosure. We want to walk close to them, but our pathway is separated from them by Plexiglas and fencing. They seem comfortable with the weather. We do not know why they are parading, but maybe it was coming close to mealtime.

Our main purpose for visiting this zoo is to give love to the Animal Kingdom of Alaska because they are no longer living free, roaming the great white land. The White Man has built concrete cities without invitation from the Nature Kingdom.

The roads are twice as wide as roads to the south. When moose and deer and other animals are crossing the roads. there is a danger they may be struck by cars. Of interest to me, in Alberta, Canada, there are special overpasses for the animals to use to avoid this danger.

After we leave the two polar bears, we come to a Golden Eagle living alone in his outside enclosure. He looks lonely. Then we come to an enclosure with one Great Horned Owl. His coat is big and fluffy and he is facing the sun. We think the sun is the radiator for the Great Horned Owl.

The zoo has several wolves of various colors and one is white. They are living in the same area as the ravens. Also living here is a small red fox curled up in a tight knot keeping warm. For heat he has stuck his nose stuck into his fur. We see two musk oxen in two large separate enclosures, and we think these animals should live together.

Our Egyptian taxi driver takes us now to an Eskimo exhibit at a local bank where we view a collection of native dress and carvings. I love the animal tusk carvings, called Scrimshaw, showing many animals figures all related.

There is a great feeling of unity among them.

The taxi driver now takes to the Alaska Native Heritage Center. Here, we slowly move through exhibits of native dress and mukluks and we come to a Native Alaskan woman sewing dance costumes for young boys and girls to wear during community celebrations. She invites us to see her fine work and then she shows us an exhibit of local basket weaving that she enjoys.

We have enjoyed touching base today with the land, with the animals with the native people. The area feels calm. We feel the weight has lifted. There will be no earthquake.

In the late afternoon, we take a nap in the sun and we send our love to the mountains, to the land, to the water, to the people -- to all of Alaska.

When the sun sets, we watch it descend. It begins after 7:00 p.m. and continues slowly until after 9:00 p.m.

We have had an amazing day in powerful, beautiful Alaska!

CHAPTER 9

Antarctica

Ｆrom Barbara:

It is June 4, and as I am writing this chapter, my thoughts are on cracks appearing on the giant ice-covered continent called Antarctica. A report has just appeared on the Internet saying that a huge crack has expanded eleven miles in six days!

An estimated 2,000 square miles of ice could break away.

In 1994, I visited Antarctica and I found the continent to be calm. The energy was good.

Today, my thought is that Antarctica is caught under great stress because the ice-covered surface is ready to give way.

To me, the continent is calling out for help. Anyone or anything under stress will call out for help.

We need to help.

In January 1994, when I visited Antarctica, my eyes saw this as virgin territory covered with ice that humans could have difficulty living on. Because humans could not live here, the continent did not have vibrations of destruction known to the human race. To me, I was visiting virgin territory.

However, the vibrations of Antarctica have suffered the consequences of depletion of the ozone layer in the earth's atmosphere. And so, I know the Antarctic vibrations I was feeling in 1994 are not exactly normal today.

I also know that in 1993, people were sent to the tip of South America who understood how to use healing fires to help correct imbalances. But, there is only so much one can do. Today it is 2017, many years after 1993, and I am reading about the ice melting and a huge crack has increased itself eleven miles in six days!

Here are my 1994 notes:

January 14, I am awake at 3:25 a.m., looking out my stateroom porthole to see floating bits of icebergs just off the Antarctic coast. I am facing the continent and I see majestic virgin, snow-covered mountains coming down to the water's edge. On the other side of the ship, I know there are snow-covered islands.

There is almost sunshine at 3:25 a.m. Yes, sunshine. It is my understanding that January is the high summer month for this part of our world.

Wouldn't this high summer month be the high breeding time for what is living on Antarctica?

Penguins live on Antarctica. They roost on stone nests. It is fun hearing them squawking when a penguin tries to steal a stone from another's nest!

I remember walking on pathways carved out by penguins going to the water. It is easier walking on their established pathways then to make a new pathway through virgin snow.

The penguins take first choice when it comes to using the pathways. One needs to step aside to allow them to waddle to the water on their pathways.

Now that their homeland Antarctica is melting, what will happen to the penguins living here? I have recently read that green is appearing in Antarctica. Penguins make their homes on snow.

More from my 1994 notes:

January 15, I am riding in a zodiac from ship to shore and we are skimming across dark blue somewhat choppy water passing several big icebergs trapped in the bay.

We land on a rocky shore that has big to middle-sized rocks, and then we are treading our way across these rocks to reach a snowy path that takes us to low nylon tents that are the living quarters of British who have come here for a technical purpose.

About fifty feet to our right, lying on the snow, is a seal. We are told not to go beyond this seal. Also, penguin rookeries to the right are to be kept completely apart from humans. But, to our left, we may go where we wish, provided we respect the penguins because they have the right of way. We must stay more then twelve feet away from them. And very definitely, we cannot disturb their roosts.

As further explanation of this command, we are told that white birds of prey are here to catch off-guard roosting penguins guarding either their eggs or their babies.

How different Antarctica is from my homeland! And I know Antarctica is different from the homelands of many others who come here.

The penguins cannot speak and so they cannot object. Yet, for their protection, I realize humans need to be aware of what is living here.

Seals are also a part of Antarctica. While walking a beach, I remember encountering three elephant seals sleeping together on the beach. As

I pass, one growls but none of the three act as if they notice me. I stop to take a photograph and this does not interest them in the least.

Well, if Antarctica becomes green because it has lost its snow and ice and the continent becomes inhabited by many humans, what will happen to the seals? Will they be able to continue sleeping on the beaches without being disturbed?

———————

I ask Margaret to channel for a plan to help stop the splitting of Antarctica.

Emma says: (Use) psychic strapping holding the continent intact. (Use) Songlines to hold the energy stable.

A place in South America stands as an anchor base to hold in place the perimeter and center of Antarctica. (This can) hold and prevent unnecessary splitting to keep stable the continent.

Provide a plate underneath to hold steady the continent and a psychic (energy) cover on top that is capped and strapped.

———————

Margaret and I ponder Emma Kunz's remarks. How can we hold steady the continent, provide a cover for it, strap it?

The Higher Worlds told us a few years ago to strap the African continent so it would not split along the lines of the Great Rift. We placed the continent in a tight stocking so there would be no give.

Well, we cannot use a stocking to hold Antarctica. However, we need to follow Emma Kunz's suggestion. We can put a 'substitute for Antarctica' on an energy plate to hold the continent steady so it will not break up. And, we can put a cover strapped across the top of the substitute continent so it will not move.

On my 1994 visit to Antarctica, I took many photographs and put them in a big photo book. This book has been sitting on a top shelf of a tall bookcase.

Maybe it has been waiting for me. In any case, I take it from the bookcase and Margaret and I follow Emma Kunz's suggestions to place this book as a substitute for Antarctica on a sturdy plate. Over the book we put plastic sheeting that is strapped top and bottom to the book. We have included a big sign -- ANTARCTICA -- so that all can easily see it.

As for Emma Kunz's suggestion to use Songlines to help stabilize the energy of Antarctica, we have investigated the use of them. David Adams has given us much information. We know that they are energy lines that run throughout the planet, including non-physical places.

We ask these energy lines to help us with the project of stabilizing Antarctica.

From Margaret:

I feel overwhelmed by trying to help Antarctica and I ask Emma for more help.

She says: Pick a line of thought and hold to that. You are concerned about the cracking of the ice cap and portions falling into the water causing the sea levels to rise and the nature of the water to change.

You have chosen to use a sacred energy place to augment the stability of the continent of Antarctica. You have symbolically stabilized a vulnerable portion and reinforced that in meditation.

Now, keep thinking calm and solidifying thoughts for the ice shelf.

Spread peace and stability outwards. Hold inner peace within. Spread this outwards for the world. Mother Earth needs these frequencies.

In meditation, I hold a cowry, a shell from Australia, to represent sea life. Also, I have three gold citrine crystals to represent land. In meditation we play Musical Rapture, Earth healing music.*

*See Glossary: Musical Rapture.

More channeling from Emma:

The Earth became crystalline in 2012 and the Sun is melting the ice and snow of the Arctic and Greenland and the ice is cracking off in Antarctica causing the oceans to rise. The interior of Mother Earth is heating up and spinning faster. The Sun has changed, becoming brighter, more crystalline in light.

We are all in higher dimensions. Time has speeded up. In the higher dimensions, the barriers of understanding, the density of reality, have diminished. Humanity can access all modalities. The lines of communication are open through crystalline clarity of Truth, accessed and shared through the vibration of Love. If one operates in a positive way for the good of the whole and all planetary systems, access to these lines of communication is available.

Heart thought communication is available with the Sun, the ocean life, the crystals and stones, the plant life, the trees, the animals, the Spirit Guides, the Angels. Everything is clearer and sharper, and words spoken need to be used in a positive manner. Lower thoughts, negative emotions, drop one into density that goes nowhere or leads to a spiral of confusion.

It is important for humans to set their mental, emotional, spiritual gauge to the higher frequencies and truth. Revenge, retaliation, blocks the systems.

So too, anger and criticism (inner and outer) lowers the vibration and turns one on one's self.

Move to focusing on Bright Words. Stand tall in perfect balance. Hold high ideals of Peace, Joy and Light. Always show the way. Give comfort. Always attend to the needs of humanity and Nature.

Barbara Wolf; Margaret Anderson

Do not fall back into self-absorption of petty ideas. Follow the large concepts of Harmony, Unification, Encouragement to right action – to spread Good Will and Love to those you meet.

Follow this and the planet will become a bright Star in the universe, shining forth its Love and its Light.

More from Margaret:

Later I am walking around the local reservoir feeling the strength of the clear sparking waters. Then I feel the presence of dolphins. Could they be swimming here with me? Now I feel the presence of the Golden Dolphins. They are with me, above me, and beyond.me. I cherish their presence and I acknowledge with love the presence of the Water Element and the dolphins.

As I continue walking, I address the ambassador tree, a very tall tree, and all the other trees that are present. It is wonderful to be here with the trees -- the Nature Kingdom.

Now I stop and face the sparkling water. I thank the water. I thank the dolphins. I thank the trees. I thank Mother Earth.

I feel refreshed. I feel the Higher Worlds are smiling.

From Barbara:

When I visited Antarctica in 1994, it was big and beautiful. The energy was good. I want that energy to return.

I am so concerned about what is happening in Antarctica, I send a message the Global Meditation Network to bring in their support.

Hello from my heart, everyone, this is Barbara Wolf.
Global Meditations Network.
http://www.globalmeditations.com

92

Perhaps you have been reading about cracks appearing in the great ice-covered Antarctica. These cracks are being closely monitored by scientists.

The Washington Post newspaper says one huge chunk of ice may be ready to break away. Thousands of square miles of ice are in this chunk. For me, having that float around would require a close watch.

What can we do to ease the potential problem of so much ice cracking away from Antarctica?

All of us have the ability to send out positive energy. We can say, "We love you, Mother Earth. We love you, Antarctica."

We will be sending out positive energy to help ease the problem.

Peace, Love, and Light,
Barbara Wolf

CHAPTER 10

Summer Solstice

From Margaret:

June 16, I will take the train to New York City to participate in Paul Winter's 22nd Annual Summer Solstice Celebration at The Cathedral of Saint John the Divine.* The weather here has been quite rainy and I am hoping that the sun will take charge when I am gone and also take charge when I am in New York City.

*See Glossary: Summer Solstice Celebration.

I am up at 3:30 a.m. to finish packing and getting organized for the trip. Joan Lenhard the taxi driver comes at 7:00 a.m. and we are soon at the train station. We wait for Train 284 which arrives on time at 8:11 a.m. and we all board by climbing high steps with the help of two train conductors.

In August, the construction of a new train station will be finished and passengers will then be able to walk straight onto the train from a new platform. That will make a big difference!

The train is medium full. The feeling tone is pleasant. All in our car are heading to Penn Station, New York City. It is cloudy and slightly cool. However, as we move along, dense fog comes in and covers the area. Because the fog blurs landscape details, trees seem more pronounced and their silhouettes seem larger, thicker, more intense. It is as if I am journeying in a *SPECIAL TREE LAND*. Native Americans call this time the Moon of the Tree.

Barbara and I are excited as we pass through Herkimer, home of the Herkimer Diamonds and Sun Disc. We were here two weeks ago, and the weather was acceptable. However, the waterways were high as we passed them and today, June 16, I notice that the waterways are even higher.

Barbara is at the window looking down, and she tells me the river is mighty close to the train tracks. We think it is the Mohawk River. We also think that if the rain continues, eventually the trains will not be able to use the tracks.

Yes, the high rivers are a worry for us. Barbara keeps telling me she sees no ducks or geese. Where are they? She wonders if prospective duck and geese parents will not breed because it is too dangerous for their babies.

Now it is time for me to sleep and I sleep deeply, not wakening until we reach Thunder Mountain far down the Hudson River. This is a very powerful mountain. Also, we are in Pete Seeger land and his focus was on cleaning up the river. His boat was named Clearwater. He is no longer with us but his crew continues his environmental efforts. Clearwater will soon be sailing to Washington, D.C. to speak about the protection of river environments.

I have been wondering why our train conductor has been announcing stops along the way so freight trains can pass. A snack bar attendant tells me that the tracks belong to the freight lines, and that is why passenger trains have to move over or stop when a freight train is passing. Also, I am realizing there is a lot of work on the rails and so there is often a single rail passage for all trains. I wonder if this rain is affecting the track beds.

But, we do make up for lost time and we do not arrive in New York too behind schedule. However, I know we will arrive Penn Station at rush hour. When we do arrive, I see the station not as crazy-packed as rush hour last year when we arrived. I am amazed that Penn Station has such few travellers now. Where are the tourists?

We take the subway to 96 Street to stay at the Days Hotel Broadway and we are given an upgrade for our room. What a nice surprise! Then, we have a delicious dinner at the Manhattan Diner. It is good to be in New York City.

Later that night, when I write up my notes, I address the Higher Worlds about my deep meditative sleep when we traveled the Hudson River in all the rain and fog.

Here are my notes:

Dear Higher Worlds, I saw a lot of water today in flooded rivers, fog over mountains, rain on the landscape. When the train turned south to travel down the Hudson River to New York City, I fell into a deep sleep. I felt I went somewhere in another reality -- a place of deep centering -- into the World of Water.

I felt a frequency of great comfort -- nurturing, creativity -- Life Force emerging. I delighted to be embraced by this powerful loving frequency. I felt the creation -- the way of water, the world of water, the merging -- the flowing, being with and becoming water. I felt totally at peace. I went deeply into the vibration of peace.

In that vibration of peace and oneness with water, I felt enormous deep love and respect and awe of water. That merging, understanding, loving of the element of Water showed me its force, its creativity, its creation of life. With this understanding, I ask the Water Element if it is appropriate for me to ask for a moderation of the excessiveness of water. There is too much rain, flooding, affecting bird life and other life forms.

I receive: The Water Element is affected when other elements such as land, air, and fire are affected by human miscreation (pollution) as well as other factors like the Sun's intensity and solar storms and the change in the Earth's core speeding up.

Humanity needs to see its place, its position in the scheme of things. You humans are on top of vast amounts of water and vast amounts of non-water. How you handle the big picture, humans, will affect the results of climate variability and changes in intensity and extremes.

Remember when the hurricane flooded New York City subways and submerged coastal highways. It took away or affected whole swaths of the eastern coastline.

The Water Element can only do so much.

Humans need to practice temperance, moderation, humility, generosity, compassion, universality. The individual ego needs to be reduced to develop a spirit of unity with the human world and the Natural World.

———————

I wake with an upset stomach.

At 1:00 a.m. Christ comes into my awareness and I receive an understanding that the stomach is matter and the Christ commands anti-matter. I am told to spread into space both the matter and anti-matter cells. Then Christ commands the storm of the anti-matter and this calms the matter. He says to spread the emotional storms of the body outward so there are great spaces between particles of matter and anti-matter. This calms the matter/anti-matter relationship.

I think on Christ's walking on the waters -- calming the storm.

———————

More Channeling:

I have been worried about climate change and now I receive information for a solution:

Changes are happening in the flow of time. Storms are increasing in intensity and in number.

Look at the spiral conch shell. It goes from a tight spiral to expand to a vast opening to live, to thrive. The way of the conch shell is to come from a tight spiral to an openness and life.

In human dealings, one cannot go against the spiral outwards of life's creativity. Be positive, work together. Life is abundance. Share equally.

The Spiritual Law of Equality.

Going inwards, backing up into the center of the spiral, brings paralysis. All things flow outwards. Give Love, give compassion. Work, live, love together.

Peace will come. AUM.

June 17, I am up early to go to The Cathedral of Saint John the Divine for Paul Winter's 22nd Annual Summer Solstice Celebration. A cab is called at 3:35 a.m. and I am soon at the Cathedral. Wonderfully, the doors are open. People were already there.

I have tickets for preferred seating and so I walk straight up to the front rows and sit in the second row to be in line with the Christ wearing red robes in a stained glass window high above. The Christ will be lit up by the rising of the sun.

Reserved seats are in front of me but these are never filled and so in reality I am in the front row. How wonderful. Now two women come to sit beside me. One is from Florida and the other, from California, tells me she is an artist who lives in a forest of great oaks and paints their portraits. I know we are connected by the love of trees.

The Cathedral darkens at 4:30 a.m., and we are in total darkness except for a few faint candle lamps above the altar. Soothing music begins reflecting Paul Winter's daily early morning meditation at a stream near his home. The sound of the water brings him peace. Now this peace is reflected by musicians beginning to play soprano sax, cello, English horn, piano, and organ. Paul Winter is playing a soprano sax. It is amazing to hear the music.

Now, the Florida Singing Sons boys choir begins singing with precise harmonies of earlier times. This lifts the frequencies to a delicate spirituality.

Later, when Paul Winters begins playing his Solstice salute, he is announcing the dawn's first light and the coming Solstice -- the longest day, the greatest Light.

Then, organist Tim Brumfield begins playing deep rumblings of dissonance, anxiety, unsettledness. It grows and grows and the negativity expands, reflecting the mood of the country and the world.

Suddenly, sunlight appears. Now the organ music changes as LIGHT breaks through in the chords and melody. HARMONY bursts forth with crushing POWER. We are all holding our breath. The POWER is so intense. The GOOD wins! The negativity is overcome. RIGHT ORDER is established once again. IN PURE JOY.

Paul Winter and my eyes lock. We smile at each other. We know what organist Tim Brumfield is doing -- cracking the negativity and sending it away in pieces to dissipate and disappear. GONE. The Sun has returned in fullness and the darkness has been overcome.

All hearts are lifted. All hearts rejoice. It is a powerful Solstice event!

I have felt Christ's presence beside me. He is here for the concert to join in the powerful positive energy of the event. I feel Paul Winter senses something special and keeps focusing in my direction. Our eyes catch and lock in the understanding that something profound was happening by the magic of the music and the hearts of the people. A deep sense of Peace arises to be felt here and sent around the world.

A sweet young female Celtic dancer dances across the stage.

After the performance, Paul Winter comes down the steps straight to me and shakes my hand. I thank him for an amazing concert. He thanks me for coming from such a long distance. I am very touched. He greets the others and is soon surrounded by many enthusiastic Solstice music lovers.

I move around and find organist Tim Brumfield to give him a great hug and tell him he did it. He cleared the negativity with powerful organ playing.

The whole concert is perfect.

I take a taxi back to the hotel and by noon I am ready for the next adventure.

From Barbara:

You have just read about Margaret's adventure at The Cathedral of Saint John the Divine when she witnesses the changing of negative energies to the positive.

Here is my message to you:

When Margaret's adventure is taking place, I am meditating alone on Floor Twelve of a large New York City building quite near The Cathedral of Saint John the Divine. It is 4:30 a.m. on June 17, 2017 and sound is being used to change negative energies to the positive.

People from far away are at the Cathedral to witness this event, and afterward they will be spreading positive energies as they return home.

The actual moment of the Solstice will be just after midnight on June 21 in New York State, and so there are only four days remaining to clean away the negative and bring in the positive.

In meditation, I am holding in my hands a photo of The Christ and three Herkimer Diamond crystals that hold the powerful positive energy field of the Herkimer Sun Disc.

Suddenly, I hear the powerful click click click of a cicada.

The sound is loud and clear.

What a surprise!

How often have I heard a cicada while meditating?

Never.

How often have I heard a cicada while not meditating?

Seldom.

How can a cicada be clicking inside a tall, tall building?

Now I realize the cicada is sending me a message about what is happening at the Cathedral.

A few years ago, I remember hearing tree frogs during Paul Winter's Solstice event inside The Cathedral of St. John the Divine. He wanted the tree frog sounds to be a part of his cleaning program.

And so, yes, now I realize the cicada is connecting to me in order to send me a message.

Paul Winter, whether or not you know this, you have reached me!

The cicada is sending me the message that the powerful Cathedral of St. John the Divine has been 'swept clean' of negative energies and overlaid by powerful positive energies. Archangel Gabriel, whose statue is outside at the top of the Cathedral, is helping.

I place these positive energies onto The Christ (who already has them) and I place these positive energies onto the three Herkimer diamond crystals in my hands. Why? Because they are connected to the powerful Sun Disc at Herkimer.

There are 144 Sun Discs around the world, and one way or another, they are all connected with each other. It is my understanding that the main Sun Disc for the world is at Roslyn Chapel, Scotland. The entities controlling this Sun Disc have known me for several years.

Now I give to the Roslyn Chapel entities the powerful positive energy coming from the cicada who is sending me this powerful energy from The Cathedral of Saint John the Divine.

I ask the Roslyn Chapel entities to send this powerful energy to the 144 Sun Dices positioned throughout the world. This Sun Disc method would be a quick and simple way to present the positive energy to ALL living on Mother Earth.

Mother Earth, you are being prepared for the Solstice!

And,,,,,thank you, cicada!!!!!

_____

From Margaret:

June 17, at noon I leave for Coney Island by taking the subway. At 59 Street I need to transfer and here I see many women dressed as mermaids. Now I learn they are going to the Mermaid Parade at Coney Island.

I feel the ocean rejoicing. I feel the WATER rejoicing. Suddenly buckets of rain fall on Coney Island. Oh well, the mermaids don't seem to mind rain.

Now I meet two sweet people, Danica and Brandon, who guide me to the New York Aquarium through all the mermaid crowds. I enter the Aquarium to give the Love and Blessings to the fish and sea life.

Especially, I go to my favorite exhibit, Glover's Reef, a large room-sized tank with viewing walls to see different species of eels, rays and silvery fish swimming in the tank.

Outside, the rain stops and I decide to go to the water, the ocean, to put down Vortex Symbols. As I am doing this, drawing the twenty-two Symbols at the water's edge, the sun comes out!!!

Now I watch as the ocean comes in and takes the Symbols.

On the beach is a beautiful shell near the drawing of the Symbol of the Universal Law of Perception. I place this shell in the center of the Symbol, and I feel Perception is the key to this gifting of the Vortexes to the Atlantic Ocean.

Sea gulls are watching, attending. Swimmers are off in a distance.

Now I ring the Blessing Chimes for the ocean.

All are connected – all are honored -- the Water, the Sun Discs, the Solstice. All are linked together. AUM.

When I return the hotel, the Sun is still shining. It is a beautiful day.

From Barbara:

Chapter 2 tells you about unicorns which, in the old days was common knowledge. But over the years, this knowledge faded.

Recently, Saint Germain has told the world that the high energy of the unicorn has begun to enter Mother Earth. This positive energy may calm matters. In ancient times, the unicorn was considered to be a symbol of purity.

Well, quite suddenly we are faced with the reality of mermaids. Margaret has encountered a Mermaid Parade filled with males and females. My thought is that, like the unicorn, the concept of the mermaid is returning.

I begin to investigate the concept of the mermaid and I learn that the Internet displays some knowledge. She is considered a water-being with the head and upper body of a female human. Of course, since she is a water-being, she has a tail. I was interested to read that Christopher Columbus said mermaids were encountered when he was sailing in the Caribbean.

Margaret and I have had one experience involving a mermaid. We have visited Asakusa, Japan, which has a shrine to a mermaid who reportedly was found in Sumida River by two fishermen. They took her to Asakusa where a temple was built for her. To this day, people from all over the world, millions of visitors, annually visit this place.

My conclusion is that perhaps, like in the old days, people may begin to include the concept of mermaids with their thoughts.

As for thoughts about where mermaids may be found, perhaps I should concentrate on speaking here about the plight of the water on this planet. All the way down on our train journey, we saw rising rivers and lakes and even farmland with water. Everything seemed flooded or close to it. Water near some train tracks brought my thoughts to feeling that if the rain does not stop, trains will have a hard time using the tracks.

I need to send powerful thoughts about weather change so the sun comes out more and more often and the rain comes less often.

As I am meditating with these thoughts, the rain stops. THE SUN COMES OUT.

From Margaret:

June 18:

It is 7:25 a.m. and I am ready to leave the hotel to take a subway to Brooklyn in order to attend the 9:00 a.m. Sunday service at the Brooklyn Tabernacle.*

*See Glossary: The Brooklyn Tabernacle.

I know that weekends can bring construction to subway lines and so a normal way of going to the Brooklyn Tabernacle may not be possible.

After I walk to the subway station, I speak with the ticket attendant who confirms there is construction and I need to follow his instructions for going to the Tabernacle.

And yes, along the way I find much confusion, but I keep reminding myself that during all this travel I must relax and enjoy the experience. I know that I am carrying Light from Paul Winter's Concert at The Cathedral of Saint John the Divine. I must give this Light to the people I meet.

At the Tabernacle, I am warmly greeted by official greeters and invited to enter. I go to my favorite area for seating and almost immediately the service begins.

Everyone rises to sing *Praise Ye the Lord, Praise God in His Sanctuary.*

Luckily, for the church audience, words to be sung are projected on overhead screens. As I am singing, I look at rows and rows of about 200 choir members singing on stage..

When we finish singing, Pastor Jim Symbala mentions that today is Father's Day and all fathers are honored. Then there is more singing followed by a welcoming of new church members. The pastor now asks where the new member were originally from, and they are from all over the world!!

The sermon given by the Pastor is about the need to be strong -- to be strong in one's faith and not to criticize but to be in unity for the greatest good. The church has many ministries -- the shelters, the prisons, the children, the ill, etc. And he mentions the choir. I feel uplifted by being in the presence of such loving people from all the nations, races and all ages.

Everyone is united in spirit.

We are asked to pray for each other, then to hold hands with each other, and then to stand together and embrace each other. It is very heart-moving and l feel the blessing and love of such powerful praying people.

When it is time to leave, a wonderful woman I call an angel guides me to a convenient way to return to my hotel. She is now on her way to visit her brother in the hospital. She says it is important to do a good deed. She knows she will be helped when she needs help and she reminds me to keep doing good deeds.

The whole trip is a beautiful experience and I remember what I earlier have been told -- *If you rush, it takes a long time. If you go with the flow, the trip goes more smoothly and moves quickly.*

I pace myself, greeting each person as special, thinking that the subways of New York are the melting pot of the world.

Yes, New York City is still amazing. Most people are basically kind.

On return to the hotel, Barbara asks me to explain my reaction to visiting the tabernacle. I say that the Brooklyn Tabernacle is so special to me because it is filled with loving people who express Love through their presence and in their Joy of singing and their devotion to their faith. All people are included. It is a place of a major uplift in the frequency of humanity. Visitors from all over the world come to share in this wonderful frequency of Joy expressed through the heart.

Yes, Brooklyn Tabernacle is a Heart Joy factory, a broadcast station sending powerful frequency of Love throughout the neighborhood, the city, the nation, the world. The merging streams of positive energy power come together today -- the crystals, the Sun Discs, the Summer Solstice Sun Celebration of Paul Winter in music.

This has been a weekend of great celebration of the uplifting of the human spirit. From the mermaids to the gifting of the Vortexes and the linking of the Sun Discs to the Crystal Power of Mother Earth expressed in her rocks, crystals and layers to the wonder of our Planet.

It has been a Blessing to be here. The generosity of the human spirit has shown brightly.

————————

From Barbara:

For those who cannot physically be at the Brooklyn Tabernacle to sing with their hearts open with love and joy, the Internet furnishes singing coming from the Tabernacle. There are many examples to choose from.*

*See Glossary: Brooklyn Tabernacle singing.

I want to add here that it is my understanding Andromeda is the original homeland of many who continually sing at the Brooklyn Tabernacle. I know those who come from Andromeda will have their hearts wide open because their hearts are mature. I learned this a few years ago and I have not forgotten.

————————

From Barbara and Margaret:

We send you our blessings and we hope you have enjoyed reading the book!

GLOSSARY

CHAPTER 1: TUCSON, ARIZONA

John H. Betts, A Guide to the Tucson Mineral Shows for First-Time Visitors, http://www.johnbetts-fineminerals.com/jhbnyc/articles/tucson.htm

SilverStar, The EarthStar Way Calendar, http://starelders.net

Chief Golden Light Eagle, THE SYMBOLS, http://www.starelders.net and http://www.starknowledgeenterprises.com/the-symbols/

Vortexes and Symbols, see extensive information at end of Glossary.

David J. Adams, Marine Meditation, http://www.dolphinempowerment.com/MarineMeditation.htm https://soundcloud.com/david-j-adams

----

CHAPTER 2: ANIMAL PEACE ENERGIES

Emma Kunz, https://www.emma-kunz.com/en/emma-kunz/

EquiCenter Inc. http://www.equicenterny.org

CHAPTER 3: MARCH EQUINOX

Songlines: David J. Adams, <u>Masters Of Shambhala 17th March 2017,</u> https://soundcloud.com/david-j-adams

Serpent Mound: Ross Hamilton, The Great Serpent Mound Book of Wonders & Mysteries.

10000 Japanese singing Beethoven's Ode to Joy (Video), https://www.youtube.com/watch?v=xBlQZyTF_LY

Musical Rapture, https://www.eraofpeace.org/musical-rapture

CHAPTER 4: WASHINGTON, D.C.

Vortexes and Symbols: See extensive information at end of Glossary, http://www.starelders.net and http://www.starknowledgeenterprises.com/11-11-symbols/

Bawa Muhaiyaddeen, http://www.bmf.org/about/bawa-muhaiyaddeen/

The Statue of Freedom, Barbara Kinney Photography, http://barbarakinney.com/blog/?p=673

CHAPTER 5: HOLY DAYS

Meditation music: Soothing Relaxation by Peder B. Helland (Video),

https://www.youtube.com/watch?v=1ZYbU82GVz4

CHAPTER 6: EARTH DAY, MAY DAY

Feel Love and Peace by Mieko Sakai (Video),

https://www.youtube.com/watch?v=5BrDIp8edP4&feature=share

Wild Wings Inc. bird sanctuary: https://www.wildwingsinc.com

CHAPTER 7: HERKIMER, HOWE CAVERNS, CONCORD

Herkimer Diamonds, http://geology.com/articles/herkimer-diamonds.shtml

Symbols and Calendar: See extensive information at end of Glossary.

http://www.starelders.net and http://www.starknowledgeenterprises.com/11-11-symbols/

Taconic Mountain formation diagram,

https://upload.wikimedia.org/wikipedia/commons/2/20/Taconic_orogeny.png

----

CHAPTER 9: ANTARCTICA

Musical Rapture, https://www.eraofpeace.org/musical-rapture

CHAPTER 10: SUMMER SOLSTICE

Paul Winter Summer Solstice Celebration, http://www.paulwinter.com/summer-solstice/

The Brooklyn Tabernacle, http://www.brooklyntabernacle.org

On the Internet, search Brooklyn Tabernacle Singing Videos, and then look for the heading, Brooklyn Tabernacle Choir Songs.

VORTEX SYMBOLS

Chief Golden Light Eagle and Grandmother SilverStar have given us valuable information on how to use powerful energy fields to help Mother Earth and all that live on her. This information has come from sacred ceremony and the information is available through:

1. THE SYMBOLS. The Universal Symbols and Laws of Creation: *A Divine Plan by Which One Can Live.*

Original title: MAKA WICAHPI WICOHAN, Universal & Spiritual Laws of Creator. [The 11:11 Symbols Book] By Standing Elk © 1996]

2. THE EARTHSTAR WAY 13-Moon Calendar, The Universal Symbols and Laws of Creation in Day by Day Living.

3. THE VORTEXES. The Universal Symbols and Laws of Creation. http://www.starelders.net and http://www.starknowledgeenterprises.com/11-11-symbols/

Here is more explanation on the Vortexes and Symbols:

Two Star Law Symbols combined make one Vortex.

The **Vortex of Light, Sound and Vibration** is formed by joining the Symbol of the *Universal Law of Light, Sound and Vibration* with the Symbol of *Spiritual Law of Intuition.*

The **Vortex of Integrity** is formed by the *Universal Law of Free Will* combining with the *Spiritual Freedom of Man*. This is a free will planet and can only operate fully when there is complete spiritual freedom of man. There should be freedom with truth and honesty.

The **Vortex of Symmetry** is formed by combining the *Universal Law of Symmetry* with the *Spiritual Law of Equality*. Symmetry means balance between all things, both spiritual and material. As above, so below. Also, equality between male/female, left/right brain, etc.

The **Vortex of Strength, Health and Happiness** is formed with the combining of the *Universal Law of Movement and Balance* with the *Spiritual Strength, Health and Happiness*. In life one has to be balanced to move forward and also one has to move forward to be balanced. Balance is symmetry in motion. With movement and balance come strength and health and happiness.

The **Vortex of Right Relationship** is produced by combining the *Universal Law of Innocence, Truth and Family* with *Spiritual Protection of Family*. This is also a powerful Vortex of social relationship (based on truth) when the concept has moved from the individual to the group.

The **Vortex of Growth** is formed when the *Universal Law of Change* is combined with the *Spiritual Growth of Man*. Change is a basic tenant of life. With spiritual growth, all things thrive. All things change. Nothing is static. Therefore, both the individual and society need the spiritual growth of man. When humanity grows spiritually, then the Vortex of Growth flourishes. In the natural state, all things grow unhindered. With spiritual growth all things thrive.

The **Vortex of True Judgment** is formed by combining the *Universal Law of Judgment* with the *Spiritual Law of Karma*. All actions should be looked at through the eyes of the *Universal Law of Judgment* so that no harm is done and there is no karma. The latter, the consequences of action, can be turned into dharma, teaching. This law applies socially as well as environmentally.

The **Vortex of Perception** is formed by the combining of the *Universal Law of Perception* combined with the *Spiritual Law of Future Sight*. It is important to perceive the impact of one's actions and to use the gift of future sight. Needed now are planetary actions that affect in a good way the lives of the people in relationship to the air, the water, the land, the life on this planet.

The **Vortex of Connection to Life** is formed with the combining of the *Universal Law of Life* with the *Spiritual Law of Choice*. Life is enhanced by correct choices. It is diminished by poor choices. Therefore, choose wisely. Choice and Life are integrally connected.

The **Vortex of True Nature** is formed by the combining of the *Universal Law of Nature* with the *Spiritual Law of Protection*. Nature exists and thrives. It is up to mankind to protect Nature so that all life thrives on this planet.

The **Vortex of Love** is formed by combining the *Universal Law of Love* with the *Spiritual Law of Healing*. One has to have Love to give healing and to receive healing. Love is the greatest healer. People, Nature, all creatures, plants, cells, molecules, atoms, adamantine particles respond to Love. All have a consciousness. Love creates. Love heals. Love is the highest power of all.

A Vortex is formed at the center of a circle of all Vortexes displayed together. This Vortex is called **Universal Unity and Spiritual Integrity**. All Vortexes bring unity. All Vortexes thrive with integrity. Integrity is the foundation of the Vortexes.

Printed in the United States
By Bookmasters